Samuel Macpherson Janney

Conversations on Religious Subjects Between a Father and His Two Sons

Samuel Macpherson Janney

Conversations on Religious Subjects Between a Father and His Two Sons

ISBN/EAN: 9783337719845

Printed in Europe, USA, Canada, Australia, Japan

Cover: Foto ©Lupo / pixelio.de

More available books at **www.hansebooks.com**

CONVERSATIONS

ON

RELIGIOUS SUBJECTS,

BETWEEN

AND HIS TWO SONS.

E Y

At a meeting of the Representative Committee, or "Meeting for Sufferings," held 5th month 17th, 1860:

After deliberate consideration of the subject, the Book Committee was authorized to purchase three hundred copies of "CONVERSATIONS ON RELIGIOUS SUBJECTS," by SAM'L M. JANNEY.

Extracted from the minutes.

WM. DORSEY, *Clerk.*

PREFACE.

The following Essays are offered to the public with a hope that they may receive a candid perusal from inquiring minds, and that they may, under the Divine blessing, lead some to examine with attention the important doctrines of which they treat, and to build their houses, not upon the sandy foundation of traditional belief, but upon the rock of immediate revelation; for on this rock only, the true church of Christ has ever been established.

The colloquial style has been chosen, in order to render the work more interesting to the young; and as affording a better opportunity of stating the objections that are generally advanced against the views here advocated.

The Author has endeavoured to state fairly the arguments of those who differ from him in opinion, and especially to bring into view those passages of scripture on which they have most relied; for he believes that these sacred records are, under Divine influence, of inestimable value in giving us a knowledge of Christian doctrines. It is, however, the principal aim of this work, to show that the kingdom of Christ is a spiritual kingdom: and that wherever it is established in the heart, it ascribes "glory to God in the highest," and promotes "peace on earth, and good will to men."

OCCOQUAN, Va., 2d mo. 24, 1835.

PREFACE

TO

THE FOURTH EDITION.

THE third edition of "Conversations on Religious Subjects," published by the late John Comly, being exhausted, it has been deemed advisable to issue a fourth edition, as the demand for them still continues. A few notes have been added by the author, to elucidate some passages not sufficiently clear in the early editions.

S. M. JANNEY.

NEAR PURCELVILLE, LOUDOUN Co., Va.,
    6th mo. 18, 1860.

CONTENTS.

CONVERSATION I.
On Repentance and Conversion............ .... PAGE 9

CONVERSATION II.
On Divine Worship........... 41

CONVERSATION III.
On the Original and Present State of Man......... 79

CONVERSATION IV.
On the Divine Being.. 111

CONVERSATION V.
On Salvation by Christ....... 155

CONVERSATION VI.
On Baptism and the Lord's Supper............. 191

(viii)

CONVERSATIONS, Etc.

CONVERSATION I.

ON REPENTANCE AND CONVERSION.

James. I feel desirous of information respecting some of the principal doctrines of Christianity;—for the great variety of opinions prevailing among the professors of religion, and the bitterness which some of them appear to feel towards others, have had a tendency to weaken my faith, and I have no doubt they have produced discouragement in the minds of many others.

Father. It must be acknowledged that a great diversity of opinion does exist upon many points of doctrine; but this should not weaken our faith in the reality of *vital religion;* for a great variety of opinions may be found among men in most departments of knowledge. The greatest philosophers have often been mistaken by founding their systems upon speculations and conjectures, instead of watching the operations of Nature, and reasoning from facts. And it is in this way that many professors of religion continue to err, by attaching too much importance to the conjectures they have formed about religion, and by attending too little to the operation of the Spirit of Truth in their own minds; by obedience to which they might become experimentally acquainted with vital religion, and "renewed in knowledge after the image of Him that created them." Notwithstanding the great variety of doctrines among the professors of Christianity, I could easily prove to you from pious and experienced writers of every sect that I am acquainted with, that they all agree in regarding true religion as a work of the heart rather than of the head; and the experience of all ages proves that "the grace of God *which bringeth salvation* hath appeared to all men, teaching us that denying ungodliness and worldly lusts, we should live soberly, righteously, and godly in this present world." The operation of this Divine Power, when it is submitted to, brings about in our minds the great change, which begins with repentance for our past sins, and ends in conversion or regeneration.

John. These are subjects on which I wish for information, for I have lately thought much about them, and I trust my heart has been in some measure weaned from the world, and engaged in the pursuit of that inheritance, incorruptible and undefiled, that fadeth not away.

Father. I am rejoiced to hear that the Lord has been so gracious to thee, my son, and that he is calling thee out of darkness into his marvellous light. He has, I trust, granted thee "repentance unto life," which is the first step in the path of righteousness. Like the passage of the children of Israel through the Red Sea, the baptism of repentance separates us from the land of Egypt, saves us from a host of our enemies, and fills the soul with joy, so that we can sing the song of Moses, and "make melody in our hearts unto the Lord." But the Israelites, after their first deliverance and rejoicing, had a great many trials to encounter, and a long journey to perform through the wilderness, until that crooked and perverse generation which *was born in Egypt*, was wasted away or consumed; and then there was a captain raised up in the midst of them, who led the new generation through Jordan (the river of judgment) into the promised land. The work of repentance was also typified by the watery baptism of John; but true saving baptism is "not the putting away of the filth of the flesh, but the answer of a good conscience towards God." 1 Peter iii. 21. And this saving baptism is administered by the Holy Spirit, which comes into the heart, and purifies or "sprinkles it from an evil conscience." Repentance is the gift of God,—and it is offered to the acceptance of all men; for all are visited with seasons of calm reflection and serious thoughtfulness, when their sins are "set in order before them," and all the pleasures of sense and the riches of this world seem "as nothing and vanity," compared with that peace of mind which they have lost while pursuing after shadows. This state of mind is sometimes experienced by those who are the most eager in pursuit of pleasure and worldly glory; but they too generally put it from them, and fly to amusements or business to drive it away. Yet this very thing which is so much shunned, is nothing less than a visitation of Divine Love, which, if yielded to, would lead to eternal salvation. It is indeed the voice of Christ, who says, "Behold, I stand at the door and knock; if any man hear my voice, and open the door, I will come in to him, and will sup with him, and he with me." Rev. iii. 20.

Those who yield obedience to this heavenly vision, not consulting with flesh and blood, will experience the baptism of repentance to take place in their souls, for "godly sorrow worketh repentance to salvation;" and the only sure evidence of sincere repentance, is bringing forth fruits "meet for repentance."

James. Does not repentance often take place without any fruits? It appears to me that I have been sinning and repenting for many years, without much, if any amendment.

Father. There is a spurious kind of repentance that scarcely deserves the name;—it does not proceed from a true sense and *hatred of sin,* but from a *dread of punishment,* which induces men very often to feel a transient regret for what they have done, and to take up resolutions to do better in future; but these resolutions, when made in man's own strength, and with a *reliance upon his own arm* for their execution, will not stand in the hour of temptation; the first gust of passion will blow them away. True repentance implies not only a godly sorrow for sin, but a turning away from it. It implies a returning again to Him from whom the soul has revolted. "Repent," says the prophet, "and turn your selves from all your transgressions: so iniquity shall not be your ruin." Ezekiel xix. 36.

John. I have no doubt that true repentance is a work of the Divine Spirit in the soul, and that it is accompanied by forgiveness of sins through the mercy of God. But I have been led to believe that the joy and peace which I have found springing up and abounding in my heart, was an evidence not only of forgiveness, but of conversion and regeneration.

Father. The term conversion is often used as equivalent to regeneration, and then it signifies a change of heart from a state of sin to a state of holiness,—a putting off the old man *with his deeds*, and putting on the new man, which is renewed in knowledge "*after the image of Him that created him.*" It was used in this sense by Jesus himself when speaking to Peter, just before he was delivered up: "Simon," said he, "Satan hath desired to have you, that he may sift you as wheat: but I have prayed for thee, that thy faith fail not; and when thou art *converted*, strengthen thy brethren." Luke xxii. 31, 32.

John. It appears from this passage, that Peter had not yet been converted; and it becomes an interesting inquiry for us all *to know* what was then the state of his experience, and how far a man may progress in religion without being thoroughly converted.

Father. Yes, it is a very interesting subject for inquiry,—and there are a number of passages in the New Testament that will throw some light upon it. It appears that Peter, long before this, had forsaken all, in order to follow Christ. He had been one of his disciples nearly three years. He had listened to his preaching and conversation, and beheld his miracles and holy example. He had himself been sent forth to preach, saying, "The kingdom of heaven is at hand," and he had been entrusted with the power of healing the sick and casting out devils. He had also been with his divine master in the hour of prayer, and stood by him on the mount of transfiguration, when "his face did shine as the sun, and his garment was white as the light," and "there came a voice from the excellent glory, saying, This is my beloved Son, hear ye him." Nor was Simon's experience altogether of an outward character; for when he confessed that Jesus was the Christ, the son of the living God, his master replied, "Blessed art thou, Simon Bar-jona; for flesh and blood hath not revealed it unto thee, but my Father which is in heaven."

Yet it appears that notwithstanding all his precious opportunities, and his ardent love for Christ, Peter had not yet been thoroughly converted.

John. I am almost ready to say, this is hard doctrine, who can bear it; for if Peter, after all this experience, had not been converted, how can one so young and weak as I, hope to attain that blessed state?

Father. Be not discouraged, my son. He who hath begun a good work in thee, is able and willing to carry it on and complete it. All he requires on thy part is, *watchfulness* to know his will, *obedience* to follow it, and *patience* to endure his righteous judgments. Every victory over sin, and every escape from temptation, is accompanied by an immediate reward of "joy in the holy spirit;" for he "feeds his flock like a shepherd, he gathers the lambs with his arm and carries them in his bosom."

Conversion does not depend upon the abundance of our knowledge, but upon the subjection of our wills to the Divine government. This brings us into a teachable, humble, childlike state;—for "except ye be converted, and become as *little children, ye shall not enter into the kingdom of heaven.*"

John. Is there any evidence in the scriptures

that Peter was not in this state, except the passage alluded to?

Father. Yes; there are several circumstances related of him, which show that he was still governed by his own will, and had not been "transformed by the renewing of his mind;"—for instance, when his master said to him, "Whither I go, thou canst not follow me now, but thou shalt follow me afterwards,"—Peter answered with much confidence, "Lord why cannot I follow thee now? I will lay down my life for thy sake." But it appears that his confidence in himself was entirely misplaced, for when the hour of trial came, he not only denied his master thrice, but "he began to curse and to swear, saying, I know not this man of whom ye speak." Mark xiv. 71.

John. Perhaps this instance of humiliating weakness came upon him in consequence of his having so much confidence in himself, that he did not continue in watchfulness and prayer.

Father. Yes, there is no doubt of it,—and there is no safety for the most experienced Christian, but in a state of continual reliance upon Divine aid, which is always afforded when rightly sought for. "God is faithful," says the apostle, "and will not suffer you to be tempted above that ye are able, but will with the temptation also make a way to escape, that ye may be able to bear it." 1 Cor. x. 13.

James. Was there no other part of Peter's conduct that indicated the state of his mind?

Father. Yes, there was. It appears that when Jesus began "to show unto his disciples, how that he must go unto Jerusalem, and suffer many things of the elders, and chief priests, and scribes, and be killed, and be raised again the third day; then Peter took him and began to rebuke him, saying, Be it far from thee, Lord; this shall not be unto thee. But he turned and said unto Peter, Get thee behind me, satan; thou art an offence unto me, for thou savourest not the things that be of God, but those that be of men." Matt. xvi. 21–23. This conduct of Peter arose from his not understanding the nature of Christ's kingdom; which can only be understood by coming under the government of the spirit of Christ. When Jesus was demanded of the Pharisees, when the kingdom of God should come, he answered them and said, The kingdom of God cometh not with observation. Neither shall they say, Lo here! or lo there! for behold, the *kingdom of God is within you"* Luke xvii. 20, 21. But although

Peter had experienced the baptism of repentance, which was typified by the watery baptism of John, he had not yet been introduced into the spiritual kingdom of Christ; for "the least in the kingdom of heaven is greater than John." Notwithstanding he had heard this doctrine preached, and seen it exemplified in the meek, non-resisting example of the Saviour, his mind was still veiled by the prejudices of education, and he expected the Messiah to reign as a temporal prince, to subdue their outward enemies, instead of waiting in prayer that his power might be *revealed in them*, to subdue their spiritual enemies. It was therefore expedient for them that he should go away, in order that the "Comforter, which is the spirit of Truth, might come and lead them into all truth." This Comforter is the manifestation of the same Divine life and light which dwelt in him; for "in him was life; and the life was the light of men: that is the true Light which lighteth every man that cometh into the world." John i. 4–9.

John. And did not Peter show that the natural man was still prevalent in him, when he took a sword and smote off the ear of the high priest's servant?

Father. I think that was a very strong evidence

that his heart had not been thoroughly brought under Christ's government, for the same spirit will always bring forth the same fruit. Now, the fruit of the Divine spirit "is love, joy, peace, long suffering, gentleness, goodness, faith, meekness, temperance: against such there is no law." Gal. v. 22.

James. I think Peter was very much like the professors of Christianity at the present day. He had not faith to *suffer with* Christ, but he was *willing to fight for him.*

Father. Yes: for he could fight without taking up the cross of self-denial. But how different was the conduct of the holy Jesus! for he "touched the servant's ear and healed it," saying, "Put up again thy sword into his place; for all they that take the sword shall perish with the sword." Matt. xxvi. 52.

James. Perhaps Peter had mistaken his master's meaning, when he told them a little before, "He that hath no sword, let him sell his garment and buy one."

Father. It is very probable he did mistake it, as he was not then in a state of mind to understand spiritual things;—but his mistake was soon corrected, for when they said, "Lord, here are *two swords,*" he replied, "It is enough;"

thereby intimating that he did not mean carnal weapons.

On considering the whole paragraph, in connection with the precepts and example of Christ, it is plain, that he intended only to warn them that a time of deep trial was approaching, when they would need the whole of that spiritual armour which was afterwards described by the apostle as the "whole armour of God." "Stand, therefore," says he, "having your loins girt about with *truth*, and having on the breast-plate of *righteousness;* and your feet shod with the preparation of the *gospel of peace;* above all, taking the shield of *faith*, wherewith ye shall be able to quench all the fiery darts of the wicked; and take the helmet of *salvation*, and the *sword* of the Spirit, which is the *word of God:* praying always with all prayer and supplication in *the Spirit*, and *watching thereunto* with all perseverance and supplication for all saints."— Eph. vi. 13–18.

These are the weapons of the Christian's warfare, and these were the weapons that Christ himself made use of. He overcame hatred by love, he conquered pride by meekness, and he triumphed over error by the spirit of Truth. He taught his disciples to resist not evil, but "when smitten on one cheek to turn the other also." "Love your enemies," said he, 'bless them that curse you, do good unto them that hate you, and pray for them that despitefully use you and persecute you." "If you love them that love you, what reward have you? do not even the publicans the same?" But "be ye perfect, even as your Father in heaven is perfect; for he maketh his sun to rise on the evil and the good, and sendeth rain on the just and on the unjust; and he is kind even to the unthankful and to the evil." These sublime precepts of Jesus were exemplified in every act of his spotless life, for "when he was reviled he reviled not again, and when he suffered he threatened not, but committed himself to him that judgeth righteously." 1 Peter ii. 23. "To this end was I born," said he, "and for this purpose came I into the world, that I should bear witness unto the truth." John xviii. 37. These glorious truths were taught in his discourses, confirmed by his example, and sealed with his blood. "As a sheep before his shearers is dumb, so he opened not his mouth," but patiently bore all the sufferings that their iniquity inflicted upon him; and his faithfulness under sufferings was not only a sacrifice acceptable to God, but also an example to us. "For," says the apostle, "what glory is it, if when ye be buffeted for your faults, ye shall take it patiently? But if, when ye *do well*, and suffer for it, ye take it patiently, this *is acceptable with God:* for even hereunto were ye called; because Christ *also suffered for us*, leaving us *an example* that we should *follow his steps.*" 1 Peter ii. 20, 21.

James. But, father, it seems to me, that if we were to follow this example and these precepts, we should be very often imposed upon and injured by the wicked.

Father. This was the very objection that the unbelieving Jews started in that day; for they said, "If we let this man thus alone, all men will believe on him, and the Romans will come and take away our place and nation." So they put him to a cruel and ignominious death; nevertheless the Romans did come, and take away their place and nation.

James. I believe most professors of Christianity expect to act upon peaceable principles, as soon as the state of the world will bear it. When the millenium shall come, then will "their swords be beaten into ploughshares, and their spears into pruning hooks; for nation shall not lift up sword against nation, neither shall they learn war any more."

John. Yes; I suppose it will be very easy to refrain from fighting, when there shall be no provocation offered to us; but how is such a state of things to be brought about?

Father. The way is very clearly pointed out,— it must be by the power of God, *manifested in the meek example and patient sufferings* of the faithful. This was the way that Christianity was first propagated; and its wonderful progress, during the days of the apostles and primitive martyrs, attests the wisdom and power of its divine Author. The apostle Peter, of whom we have been speaking, after that the Holy Spirit with power from on high had come upon him, and renewed his heart, could then follow the meek example and holy precepts of Christ; and by preaching with boldness, and suffering with patience, even unto death, he bore testimony to the truth of the Gospel, and proved that his heart was then converted by the purifying influence of the spirit of Christ. In those primitive times, the law of love governed the lives of the followers of Christ, and influenced all their conduct, not only towards one another, but towards all mankind: they did not fight against their enemies, but prayed for them. And whenever primitive Christianity shall prevail in the world, it must bear the same fruits of meekness and love; for the tree will always be known by its fruits—"men do not gather grapes of thorns, nor figs of thistles."

John. It appears to me that if all who profess to be followers of Christ would only walk in his footsteps, the world would soon wear a different aspect from what it now does.

James. I do not profess to be a religious man, but I can plainly see the great disparity there is between the profession and the practice of those who are called the followers of Christ; and I have at times been almost ready to conclude, that there is no genuine religion among them.

Father. There is no doubt that the cause of Truth has sustained more injury from the inconsistency of its professors, than from all the efforts of deists and infidels. But we must not charge upon Christianity the faults of those who merely profess the name, without becoming obedient to the spirit of Christ; for in these is fulfilled the prophecy of Isaiah, "In that day shall seven women take hold of one man, saying, we will eat *our own bread* and wear *our own apparel:* only let us be called by thy name, to take away our reproach." They do not depend upon Christ to give them the living bread which comes down from heaven, and gives life to the soul;—nor do they wait for the water of life, which springs up in the obedient, dedicated mind;—neither do they wear the seamless garment of simplicity and truth: but they are willing to be called by his excellent name, while in their hearts they are "crucifying to themselves the Son of God afresh, and putting him to an open shame."

John. Would not a continual obedience to the teachings of Divine grace in our hearts, lead us into conformity with the example of Christ?

Father. Certainly it would: for that grace is a manifestation of the same spirit that was in Christ; (John i. 4–16) and if we were obedient to it, we should be led out of all evil, and from under the bondage of corruption, into the glorious liberty of the sons of God.

James. But if this spirit is so very powerful, why is it that so few persons understand and obey it?

Father. Because, in its first appearance, the seed of the kingdom is so small that it is overlooked or trodden down. It is likened to a "grain of mustard seed, which is the smallest of all seeds, but when it is grown it is the greatest of herbs, so that the fowls of the air lodge in its branches." Those who are looking for great things, and extraordinary illuminations, will not put their faith in this little seed which is sown in every heart; and yet, " in it are hidden all the treasures of wisdom and knowledge;" for it is that " grace of God which bringeth salvation, and hath appeared to *all men*, teaching us, that, denying ungodliness and worldly lusts, we should live soberly, righteously, and godly in this present world." Titus ii. 11, 12.

The first appearance of this Divine grace, or monitor, in the hearts of transgressors, is in the character of a *reprover for sin ;*—and if we will be obedient to it, by repenting and *turning away* from our sins, it then becomes known to us as a *comforter in righteousness :*—and if we still continue to follow it for our guide, it will become to us a "spirit of judgment, and a spirit of burning, and will purely purge away our dross, and take away our tin : for Zion shall be redeemed with judgment, and her converts with righteousness." Isaiah iv. 4, and i. 25, 27.

If any man think to be saved by a profession of religion, or an implicit belief in the doctrines of Christianity, without experiencing a regeneration and bringing forth the fruits of the spirit of Christ, he is deceiving himself, and building "his house upon the sand." It was against such professors that the wo was denounced by the prophet,—"Wo unto him that buildeth his house by unrighteousness, and his chambers by wrong, that useth his neighbour's service without wages, and giveth him not for his work." Jer. xxii. 13.

John. But does not this strike at the root of involuntary slavery, which many professors are concerned in; for that appears to me to be "*using our neighbour's service without wages?*"

Father. Certainly it does: for the Jews were taught by Jesus in the parable of the good Samaritan, to regard all men as their neighbours,—even the Samaritans with whom they had long been at enmity. But there are some of his precepts which are still more pointed against slavery. One of them is, "Thou shalt love thy neighbour as thyself." And another is, "Do unto others as thou wouldst that they should do unto thee." He who follows these precepts cannot possibly compel his fellow-creatures to work for him against their consent, nor without giving them full compensation for their labour.

John. But I have heard professors who were

slave-holders say, that the Jews under the old law were allowed to hold slaves.*

Father. Yes; but Paul says "the law made nothing perfect, but the bringing in of a better hope did, by which we draw nigh unto God." Heb. vii. 19. The law of Moses was not from the beginning, but "was added because of transgression, till the seed should come to whom the promise was made." Gal. iii. 19. The Israelites were then in such a dark, carnal state, that they could not receive a more spiritual law; and the professors of Christianity whose minds are now in the same dark state, find it very convenient to go back to those who lived under the law, for examples to follow, instead of following after Christ. By this means they might justify not only war and slavery, but polygamy and other gross evils. Moses allowed a man who was not satisfied with his wife, to give her a writing of divorcement, and put her away; but Christ says, it was "*not so from the beginning,*" and that it was allowed by Moses "because of the hardness of their hearts."

---

* The permission granted to the Israelites to buy bondmen from among the heathen, was coupled with provisions for their religious instruction, and their liberation on the year of jubilee.

John. But does not the New Testament speak of *servants?*

Father. Yes: it speaks of those whose *calling* or business in life was that of servants; and Paul advises such to be content in their calling: saying, "Let every man remain in the *calling* wherein he was called. Art thou called being a servant? care not for it." 1 Cor. vii. 20. But we are not to suppose that these were slaves, for a man may agree to serve another for wages, and then he is called a servant.

John. It appears to me that a great many good men, in all ages of the world, have been concerned in the practice of going to war, and holding slaves.

Father. A great many persons who were sincerely pious, have been partakers of these evils, their eyes being so blinded by the prejudices of education that they did not see them in their true light. We find, however, that such persons have always mourned over the calamities of war, and endeavored to mitigate the hardships of slavery; and if they had followed still further the teachings of this benevolent spirit, they would have been led by it entirely out of these evils; for, like the dawning of light upon the natural world, the perception of Divine Truth in the minds of individuals and nations, is always gradual and progressive. But it appears from the history of the Christian Church, that the practice of war, even in self-defence, was condemned by the primitive Christians for the first three centuries: and after the visible church became corrupted, and had apostatized from the Truth, there were *large* numbers, in almost every age, who bore a faithful testimony against the shedding of human blood,—against oaths of every kind,—against priestcraft and persecution,—and against many of the corruptions in faith and practice which had crept into the church.

There were great numbers of these dissenters in Italy, from the ninth to the thirteenth century, who bore the name of Paterines; and a similar people were known in Piedmont by the name of Waldenses, who continued for five or six centuries, till about the time of the Reformation.* The Moravian brethren professed nearly the same principles both before and since the Reformation, and the Society of Friends have borne the same testimonies for nearly two hundred years past. All these people suffered se-

---

* For a full account of these people, see Jones's Church History. Some notice of them may be found in Mosheim's Ecc. History.

verely from persecution, and immense numbers sealed their testimonies with their blood in martyrdom, rather than take up the sword in self-defence; but they were sometimes wonderfully preserved, and seldom suffered from any others than the false professors of Christianity. Even the Indians of North America respected the Friends and Moravians, although in the first settlement of Pennsylvania they were entirely unprotected by arms, and professed the principle of non-resistance.

These holy and benevolent principles must prevail more generally among professing Chrissians, before that happy era can arrive when the lion and the lamb shall lie down together, when the outcasts of Israel shall be gathered, and Ethiopia shall stretch forth her hands unto God.

Every one who professes to be a follower of Christ, in this enlightened age, should reflect deeply upon these things, and endeavor to walk in the narrow path of self-denial; for we shall not be judged by the measure of knowledge that was imparted to *other men* of former ages, but according to what *has been made known to ourselves.* "Unto whomsoever much is given, of him shall be much required: and to whom men have committed much, of him they will ask the more." Luke xii. 48. If the holy men who are mentioned in the Old Testament lived up to the law that was given to them, we ought likewise to live up to the law that was given to us, which is not an outward law that can take cognizance of outward acts only, but is an inward law that takes hold *of the motives and principles of action*, being written by "the spirit of the living God, not in tables of stone, but in the fleshly tables of the heart." Jer. xxxi. 33, and 2 Cor. iii. 3. It is this "law of the spirit of life in Christ Jesus which makes free from the law of sin and death." See Rom. viii. 2. For it will (in those who are obedient to it) "crucify the flesh with its affections and lusts."

When the "love of God is shed abroad in the heart" and becomes our governing principle, it makes us love all God's creation, and especially all mankind; "for he made of one blood all nations of men, for to dwell on all the face of the earth."

If God is "good even to the unthankful and to the evil," will not his Holy Spirit prompt us to pursue the same course? And if his beloved Son laid down his life for the good of mankind, and prayed for his persecutors, will not his do-

c

minion in our hearts be attested by the same kind of fruits?

These truths are undeniable; and I think it is equally clear that the man who comes fully under the government of Divine Love, will not only bear a faithful testimony against all contention, oppression and injustice, but against everything that is opposed to the peace and happiness of man. He cannot enrich himself by dealing in that which makes other men poor; neither can he become an instrument of evil by encouraging in any way the frequent or unnecessary use of ardent spirits, when he sees how many thousands in our country are falling a prey to intemperance, and how many tens of thousands it has reduced to misery and ruin.

John. I should think the effect of true religion must be, not only to restrain us from evil, but to lead us into all goodness.

Father. Certainly it is. We must not only "cease to do evil," but we must "learn to do well," and thus obtain the fulfilment of that blessed promise: "Though your sins be as scarlet, they shall be as white as snow, and though they be red like crimson, they shall be as wool." Isa. i. 16–18.

Our holy and blessed example, Christ Jesus,

went about continually doing good;—it was his meat and his drink to do his Father's will; and all those who would be his disciples must follow his steps, as far as light and ability are afforded.

"Is not this the fast which I have chosen," saith the Lord, "to loose the bands of wickedness, to undo the heavy burdens, and to let the oppressed go free, and that ye break every yoke? Is it not, to deal thy bread to the hungry, and that thou bring the poor that are cast out to thy house? When thou seest the naked that thou cover him, and that thou hide not thyself from thy own flesh." Isaiah lviii. 6, 7.

He who does these things from the pure motive of Christian charity, will not sound a trumpet before him, but will endeavour to "do them in secret, and he who seeth in secret will reward him openly." It is true, the Divine Being looks at the *state of our hearts*, and the *motives* of our actions, rather than the actions themselves; but pure motives and good feelings cannot long exist in us, without bringing forth their appropriate fruits;—therefore the apostle James says, that "faith without works is dead," and that "pure religion and undefiled before God and the Father is this: to visit the fatherless and widows in their affliction, and to keep ourselves unspotted from the world." Now in order to keep ourselves unspotted from the world, we must not only forsake its vices, but we must turn away from its vain fashions and trifling amusements. We must not "be conformed to this world, but transformed by the renewing of our minds." Rom. xii. 2. And we are required "to walk in wisdom towards them that are without, *redeeming the time;* and let your speech be always with grace, seasoned with salt, that ye may know how ye ought to answer every man." Colos. iv. 5, 6.

These are the genuine and invariable fruits of being "born again of incorruptible seed, by the word of God which *liveth* and abideth forever;" and it is not possible for any soul to participate in the joys of heaven, either here or hereafter, without being born again, and made a "partaker of the Divine nature."

The gospel of Christ (by which I mean the "power of God unto salvation," Rom. i. 16,) is truly a glorious gospel; for it saves men from the dreadful effects of sin, not by an imputative righteousness, but by taking away the sinful nature out of the heart, so that those who have been dead in sin are raised up in newness of life. We cannot be reconciled to God while we remain in a state of sin; for "what communion hath light with darkness, and what concord hath Christ with Belial?" That corrupt nature *in man* which has sinned, must be crucified and slain, (Rom. vi. 6,) in order that Christ may reign in us; for "if any man be in Christ he is a new creature, all old things are done away, and all things are new, and all things of God." We must " put off the old man with his deeds, and put on the new man, which is renewed in knowledge after the image of him that created him, where there is neither Greek nor Jew, circumcision nor uncircumcision, Barbarian nor Scythian, bond nor free; but Christ is all, *and in all.*"

The true Christian knows no distinction of party or sect, of rank or condition; for he loves all mankind;—and all those who are governed by the same pure spirit, whatever may be their name or profession of religion, he can salute as brethren. He does not expect the fellowship of the gospel to be always accompanied by an entire uniformity of opinion, for it is "*the unity of the spirit*" that is "the *bond of peace;*" and if all the professors of religion were governed by that one pure spirit which speaks "peace on earth and good will to men," there would be no occasion for creeds to define the boundaries that separate one sect from another. It has always been the effect of human creeds and systems of religion, to array sect against sect, and brother against brother; but our Divine Master has given us no creed to bind the consciences of men, except the one rule by which their *principles* may be known, which is to try them by their *fruits;* for a good tree cannot bring forth evil fruit, nor an evil tree good fruit.

"Love is the fulfilling of the law," and "by this shall all men know that ye are my disciples, if ye have love one to another." "Not every one that saith unto me Lord, Lord, shall be saved, but he that *doeth the will of my Father* which is in heaven."

Let no man think himself converted, or regenerated, until he finds the pure spirit of Divine Love to be his *governing principle* in thought, word, and deed, so that "whether he eats, or whether he drinks, or whatsoever he does, it is all for the glory of God." Then, and not till then, can it be truly said that he is renewed in the spirit of his mind, and that he has put on the new man, which after God is created in righteousnes and true holinesss."— Ephesians iv. 24. We are assured that those who arrive at this blesssed state will find "the yoke made easy and the burden light," for there will be a spring of joy opened in their hearts, that will make every trial and affliction seem as nothing, for Christ's sake. The pleasures and honours of the world will, in their view, lose all their charms to please, and they will go on their way rejoicing in a living foretaste of those celestial joys which the world can neither give nor take away. But even in this state of mind, there is a continual need of reliance upon Divine aid, for "it is not in man that walketh to direct his steps." Jer. x. 23. And that solemn injunction of Christ should never be forgotten,—" Watch ye therefore, for ye know not when the master of the house cometh, at even, or at midnight, or at the cock-crowing, or in the morning; lest coming suddenly he find you sleeping. And what I say unto you, I say unto all, Watch." Mark xiii. 35.

CONVERSATION II.

ON DIVINE WORSHIP.

John. In a former conversation the subjects of repentance and conversion were discussed, and we were shown the necessity of being "born again of incorruptible seed, by the word of God, which liveth and abideth forever." There is another subject of much interest which I desire to understand, and that is the right mode of worshipping the Divine Being.

Father. This is a subject of deep interest to every awakened mind, and I shall endeavour to state my views upon it for your serious consideration; not wishing you to adopt them any further than you may be convinced in your own minds of their truth.

James. There is a wide difference among Christians of various denominations in their manner of worship, and yet most of them profess to derive their views from the same source. The Catholics have their stated forms of prayer and praise, many of which are repeated in a dead language; the Episcopalians have theirs all written and repeated in the English language; the Presbyterians have no forms for their prayers, but their hymns are set to music, and sometimes accompanied by the organ; the Methodists and Baptists have mostly discarded the instrumental music, but still retain the vocal,— while the Friends, or Quakers, have relinquished both, and all set forms of prayer and preaching, deeming neither indispensable to Divine worship, which they believe may be acceptably performed in silence. Now, if the Bible be so perfect a rule as is generally stated, how is it that all these people differ so much in their views, for they all appeal to it for authority?

Father. The Old Testament is very explicit in stating the form of worship and all the ceremonies enjoined upon the Jews, because that was an outward dispensation, intended to typify and lead to a spiritual dispensation; and its end being accomplished, it was abrogated by the coming of Christ. Now we may remember he said to the woman of Samaria, "The hour cometh and now is, when the true worshippers shall worship the Father in spirit and in truth, for the Father seeketh such to worship him.

God is a spirit, and they that worship him, must worship him in spirit and in truth."

I have no doubt that this spiritual worship,—this communion of the soul with the Father of spirits,—has been, and still is performed at times by the pious and sincere worshippers in all the various sects of Christendom;—the question is, which of the various forms of worship is most consistent with the Christian dispensation, and best adapted to promote true spiritual worship.

John. I think it is much to be regretted, that the writers of the New Testament were not a little more explicit in regard to the manner of worship, for there has been a great deal of disputing about it among the professors of Christianity.

Father. I do not think so. For Christ said to his disciples, " I have yet many things to say to you, but ye cannot bear them now; howbeit, when he, the Spirit of Truth, is come, he will guide you into all truth : for he shall not speak of himself, but whatsoever he shall hear, that shall he speak : and he will show you things to come. He shall glorify me, for he shall receive of mine, and shall shew it unto you." John xvi. 12-14. Was it not much better to direct their attention to the teachings of the Spirit of Truth, (which he has promised to all those who wait upon him) than to give them verbal or written instructions about the manner of worship, which perhaps they were not in a state to receive?

John. Those who were to be guided by the Spirit of Truth, or indued with a miraculous gift of the Holy Ghost, did not need such particular directions, but if the apostles, while under the influence of this power, had written a more minute account of their forms of worship, it might have saved a great deal of controversy.

Father. True spiritual worship does not depend upon any form, but upon the power or influence under which it is performed. "The kingdom of God is not in word, but in power." 1 Cor. iv. 20. It is not necessary that we should use the same form of worship that the apostles did,—but it is absolutely necessary that we should be governed and influenced by the same power, or Spirit of Truth; for without it we cannot even *think a good thought*, much less can we perform acceptably the solemn service of Divine worship. The apostle Paul said, "We are not sufficient of ourselves, *to think any thing as of ourselves*, but our sufficiency is of God, who also hath made us able ministers of the New Testament; not of the letter, but of the spirit; for the letter killeth, but the spirit giveth life." 2 Cor. iii. 5, 6.

John. But would not the same spirit always lead into the same form?

Father. It will always produce the same *fruits of holiness*, but not always the same form of worship; for the Divine Being adapts his instructions and requisitions to the state of the people whom he visits. His mercy and his condescension to the children of Israel were so great that he gave them an outward law, adapted to their weak, carnal state; and he made that law a figure, or shadow of good things to come, so that they might be led by the shadow to seek for the "substance, which is Christ." It is evident that the prophets and other holy men who lived under the law, did come to the knowledge of Christ; for the apostle Peter says expressly, that " the spirit of Christ was in them." 1 Peter i. 11. But in process of time, the Mosaic law became much corrupted by the traditions of the elders which the scribes had engrafted upon it, and the people became so dependent upon outward observances that they "omitted the weightier matters of the law, judgment, mercy, and faith." Matt. xxiii. 23. Then it became necessary to abolish that law, and Jesus Christ came to "take away the handwriting of ordinances, and to introduce a more spiritual dispensation, which he exemplified in his life and sealed by his death. This law of the new covenant was predicted by the prophet Jeremiah, who says, "This shall be the covenant I will make with the house of Israel: After those days, saith the Lord, I will put my law in their inward parts, and *write it* in their hearts, and will be their God, and they shall be my people." Jer. xxxi. 33. It is far superior to any outward law, because it is always adapted to the condition of each individual, and it is not limited in its application *to our outward actions,* for it condemns every evil thought which rises in the mind; and thus in the obedient, dedicated soul, it lays the axe to the root of the corrupt tree.

John. I acknowledge all this is consistent with the scriptures; but I have sometimes met with persons who say that all immediate revelation has ceased, and that we have nothing to depend on now, but the scriptures and our reasoning powers.

Father. Yes, there are such persons, and some of them even pretend to be Christians. But the scripture tells us, "No man can say that Jesus is Lord, *but by the Holy Ghost.*" 1 Cor. xii. 3.

James. I have often heard such persons speak on religion,—and I confess that I have so little knowledge on the subject, that I could not refute their reasonings. I should like to be certain that the Divine spirit does operate upon man, and inform him of his duty, before we proceed further in the consideration of spiritual worship.

Father. The best way, and the *only sure way* for a man to be satisfied of this, is, to be obedient to every manifestation of duty in his own mind,—to keep all his passions in subjection, and to do every thing that he believes will be pleasing in the sight of God; and he will then find, as he continues to walk in this path, that his spiritual perceptions will improve; and he will see many things to be wrong, which he once considered indifferent, and will experience many joys to spring up in his heart, which before were unknown to him; until at length he may arrive at that state of "full age," which the apostle Paul speaks of, "even of those who by reason of use have *their senses exercised to discern both good and evil.*" Heb. v. 14. That we have a *sense of duty*, or *moral faculty* (by some called conscience) placed in our minds, which when divinely enlightened, enables us to discern both good and evil, without *waiting for the slow deductions of reason*, must be acknowledged by every man that is acquainted with his own heart. This important truth, which is so plainly taught in the sacred writings, and so readily acknowledged by every unprejudiced mind, was long obscured, and even denied, in the false theology of the schoolmen " who darkened counsel by words without knowledge;"—but it is now acknowledged by the most distinguished writers on moral philosophy; and it has been ably proved, that this "moral sense" is one of the earliest faculties developed in childhood; that it is capable of being improved by use, or impaired by neglect; and that on its use or abuse is dependent the happiness or misery of man.*

James. These facts are acknowledged even by those who deny the authority of the scriptures.

Father. Now, if it be admitted that we have a "moral sense," for discerning between good

---

* See Stewart's Moral Philosophy.

and evil, it follows as a necessary consequence, that there must be *a medium* by which this sense is brought into use: for the *eye cannot see without light;* nor can *the ear hear without sound.* The Divine Spirit is the medium which conveys to our conscience, or *moral sense,* the knowledge of spiritual things. It is called the *light,* because it is the *medium of perception.* It is called the *word* of God, because through this medium he speaks to the soul; and it is called the *grace* of God, because it is given freely, "without money and without price."— Jesus refers to the conscience as the eye of the soul, when he says, "If thine eye be single, thy whole body will be full of light: but if thine eye *be evil,* thy whole body will be full of darkness." There is such a striking analogy between the effects of light upon the natural eye, and the operations of the Divine Spirit in the soul, that I am willing to pursue it further.

The first thing that strikes the attention of an infant is the light; yet it has no knowledge of the nature and properties of light, nor the uses for which it was designed;—it does not even know the distance, nor size, nor quality, of any thing it sees, until its senses are improved by exercise. Persons who were born blind, and have been restored to sight by a surgical operation, have at first to examine and handle every thing they see, like the infant does, until by experience they learn to judge of the size and distance of objects. All their first perceptions are imperfect and indistinct. Like the man who was restored to sight by our Lord, they see "men as trees walking." Yet none of these facts induce us to doubt of the qualities of light being the same in every individual; and even the man whose eyes are impaired by disease, so that he cannot direct his steps aright, must acknowledge, that on other men the light may be shining unimpaired.

It is thus that our mental vision becomes gradually accustomed to the influence of the Divine Spirit "in whom we live, and move, and have our being;" and as we are earnestly engaged in attending to its discoveries, and faithfully concerned to walk in the light, we shall become "children of the light and of the day," and will experience an advancement in the truth, and in the knowledge of the Lord: so that what was at first as "the light of the moon, shall become as the light of the sun, and the light of the sun shall become sevenfold, as the light of seven days: for the path of the just is as the shining light, that shineth more and more unto the perfect day."

James. I have long been acquainted, in some measure, with the effect of conscience in restraining me from doing evil, or reproaching me for it; but I had no idea that this was any thing extraordinary.

Father. It is not anything extraordinary, for all men have it; and the Divine light shines on the moral sense of all, but all men do not attend to it; for "men love darkness rather than light, because their deeds are evil."

It is acknowledged by all, that man has nothing good in his own nature, independent of the Divine Being. "There is none good but one,—that is God." Therefore, if we find any thing in our own hearts to condemn us for evil, it must be something that is good,—something that comes from God; for evil will not condemn evil. Satan is not "divided against himself." This pure principle of Divine Light not only condemns us for evil, and "sets our sins in order before us, but it likewise incites us to goodness; and when we are obedient to it, we are sensible of a holy joy, a heavenly serenity of mind, which the apostle Paul describes as the "love of God shed abroad in the heart."

John. I can bear witness to that; for I have experienced it in some measure, and I must acknowledge that it far surpasses all the joys this world can afford.

Father. These truths are admitted by the most pious and enlightened writers of every Christian denomination that I am acquainted with; and many of them have acknowledged, that at times they have been so influenced by Divine grace in their religious services that their words seemed to come to them unsought, and were accompanied with such convincing power and Divine energy, that all opposition was subdued, and many hearts were melted into love and tenderness. Almost every pious and experienced Christian will acknowledge, that he has often known something of this heavenly influence to pervade his mind, during his seasons of *private devotion,* when he has withdrawn his mind from the world, and prostrated his whole soul in silent adoration before that awful Being whose presence fills infinity, and whose power upholds the universe. Why then should there be so little of this power and this precious solemnity experienced in the religious worship that generally prevails in Christendom? Is it not because men have "forsaken God, the fountain of living water, and have hewn out to themselves cisterns,—broken cisterns, that can hold no water?" Instead of waiting for his power to influence their hearts, to control their thoughts, and to enable them to worship in spirit and in truth, how many rush into forms and ceremonies, without waiting for any Divine influence to pervade their minds; forgetful of the apostolic declaration, that we "know not what to pray for as we ought, but the spirit itself maketh intercession for us with groanings which cannot be uttered; and he that searcheth the heart knoweth what is the mind of the Spirit, because he maketh intercession for the saints according to the will of God." Romans viii. 26, 27.

John. But it will not be safe, from this, to conclude that all vocal utterance of prayer or praise is inconsistent with true spiritual worship; for Christ himself prayed with his disciples, and gave them a form of prayer at their request. It is also said that they sang a hymn after eating the passover.

Father. I would by no means restrict Divine worship to entire silence; for it does not consist in outward silence alone, any more than it does in words. The apostle Paul says, "I will pray with the spirit and with the understanding also: I will sing with the spirit and with the understanding also." 1 Cor. xiv. 15. From this it is evident he thought the understanding alone was not sufficient without the aid of "the spirit" of Divine grace, to dictate prayer or praise to God. In his epistle to the Ephesians, he tells them to "take the helmet of salvation, and the *sword of the Spirit, which is the word of God;* praying always with all prayer and supplication, *in the spirit,* and *watching thereunto,* with all perseverance, and supplication for all saints." In nearly all the instructions of the blessed Jesus and his apostles respecting prayer, the duty of *watching* is carefully enjoined; for the hearts even of the faithful, are not always in a state suited to pray or sing praises to God.

It is the duty of all to *watch thereunto,* as the "sick and the impotent folk" waited at the pool of Bethesda, until "an angel came down and troubled the water," and then "they stepped in" and "were healed of whatsoever disease they had." John v. 4.

"Watch and pray," said Jesus, 'for ye know not the hour when the Son of man cometh." "Blessed are those servants whom the Lord, when he cometh, shall find watching: verily, I say unto you, that he shall gird himself, and make them to sit down to meat, and will come forth and serve them." Luke xii. 37.

As to the hymn which they sang after eating the passover, I have no doubt it was dictated by the "power and wisdom of God," which dwelt in Jesus; for he told them on several occasions, "Whatsoever I speak, even as the Father said unto me so I speak." "I can of mine own self do nothing; as I hear I judge." Therefore a hymn, dictated and sung under this Divine influence, must have been highly edifying. When he promised his disciples that the "Comforter, which is the Spirit of Truth," should come and teach them all things, he certainly did not intend to limit its operations by confining them to a set form of prayer or praise.

The prayer known by the name of the Lord's prayer, was also dictated by the same Divine wisdom, and was exactly adapted to the occasion on which it was given; but it does not follow that it will suit all occasions; for we have no account of its being used afterwards by the apostles, although their praying is often mentioned.

The Lord's prayer is remarkably short, and yet very comprehensive; and it appears to have been designed to show his disciples, that they must not be like the heathen, who thought "to be heard for their much speaking." His parable of the publican who smote his breast, and said, "God be merciful to me a sinner," and came down justified rather than the Pharisee who made a long profession, was also intended to show, that it is not the formal hypocrite, but the humble contrite heart, which is acceptable in the Divine sight. God looks at the heart; the *form* of prayer or praise is nothing in his sight; but the influence under which it is performed is every thing. Our Lord says, "Your Father knoweth what things ye have need of before ye ask him." He knows what will be good for us better than we do ourselves; and if we set about asking him for whatever we may deem right in our own eyes, we shall often "ask amiss," and then it will be an evidence of his mercy not to grant it.

James. What is the use of praying, then?

Father. The object of prayer is *not to change the Divine purposes*, but to conform our wills to his. His will and his purposes are always the same, and *always right;* for in him is neither variableness nor shadow of turning. One object of religious worship is, to seek for light from him to *know our own states and conditions;* and when we are thus brought to see what we stand in need of, he gives us ability to ask it; he extends his holy sceptre, and *grants the prayer that is made according to his will.* This is the prayer of faith that is always availing, whether it be uttered vocally, or only breathed in the secret of the soul. The man whose heart is devoted to God will be always " watching unto prayer," and may therefore be said to " pray without ceasing," for he will be often engaged in mental supplication, or in songs of praise, " making melody in his heart unto the Lord." Nor will his prayers be confined to supplications for his own soul. As all the members of the true Church are one in spirit, being baptized by one spirit into one body, and thereby made to sympathize one with another; so each member will be at times dipped into a feeling of near unity with the brethren, and may feel himself constrained, by the influence of Divine love, to offer up a petition on their behalf, either vocal or mental, which will be acceptable in the Divine sight; and being accompanied by the influence of his Holy Spirit, cannot fail to do good. He who prays, preaches, or sings, without this influence, is like one who shoots his arrows at a venture, and, unless his rashness be overruled by Divine Providence, he is more likely to do harm than good. But even when we think ourselves clothed with ability for religious services, it is well to remember the caution of the royal preacher, "Keep thy foot when thou goest to the house of God, and be more ready to hear than to give the sacrifice of fools: for they consider not that they do evil. Be not rash with thy mouth, and let not thy heart be hasty to utter any thing before God: for God is in heaven and thou upon earth; therefore let thy words be few." Ecc. v. 1, 2.

John. Does not our Lord promise that "whatsoever ye shall ask in my name, that will I do?"

Father. Yes: there is such a promise frequently repeated: but we are not to understand that merely taking the name of Jesus Christ into our *mouths*, will ensure acceptance to our prayers; for the wicked can do this as readily as the righteous, and even those who are comparatively good may do it improperly. The name of the Lord is often used in the scriptures to signify the power, spirit, or presence of the Lord. Thus, when he promised to send his angel to go before the Israelites to keep them in the way, he told them, " Beware of him and obey his voice, provoke him not; for he will not pardon your transgressions, for *my name is in him.*" Ex. xxiii. 21. " In all their afflictions he was afflicted and the *angel of his presence saved them;* in his love and in his pity he *redeemed* them, and he *bare them and carried* them all the days of old." Isaiah xiii. 9. The prophet Jeremiah, in speaking of the coming of Christ, says, " This is *his name* whereby he shall be called, the *Lord our righteousness.*" And it is also said, " They shall call *his name* Emmanuel, which, being interpreted, is *God with us.*" Matt. i. 23.

The name Jesus (a saviour) and Christ (anointed,) was given to him, because in him dwelt a full manifestation of the " power and wisdom of God," who is the only Saviour; for he says by the mouth of the prophets, " I, even I, am the Lord, and besides me there is no Saviour." Isaiah xli. 3 and 11. Hosea xiii. 4. Now if this name is intended to signify the power, spirit, or presence of God, do not those who invoke the name without feeling the power, take the name of the Lord in vain? They who pray under the influence and direction of this holy name or power, will ask for nothing inconsistent with the Divine will, and therefore their prayers will be always availing.

John. But are we not required to pray for all men? and yet we believe that all men are not saved, for many continue to live in wickedness.

Father. God has no pleasure at all " that the wicked should die, but that he should return from his ways and live." Ezek. xviii. 23. He furnishes every man with the means of salvation; for " the grace of *God, which bringeth salvation,* hath appeared to all men." He who loves God, will love all God's creation; and this feeling of universal love will be found to arise in mental supplication for all men, that they may come to a knowledge of the same blessed truth; and sometimes these aspirations will become so earnest as to give rise to the utterance of vocal prayer, which may, under the Divine blessing, produce in others the same kind cf feelings. But these precious feelings may spread from heart to heart, and rise into dominion, *without the use of words;* for there is in Divine love a sympathetic influence, which pervades the minds of those who worship aright; and when they are assembled together in worship, it brings them into the " unity of the spirit, in the bond of peace," and they seem to live and breathe in an atmosphere of love. This holy influence may be felt in such a degree as to surpass the power of utterance; for human language has no terms by which to convey it to others, and it can only be conveyed in that "language in which we were born," which is the language of impressions made upon the heart by the finger of God. The same kind of holy solemnity is described in the Revelations, as the highest degree of religious worship; for, after the opening of the sixth seal, the apostle "saw a great multitude which no man could number, of all nations, and kindreds, and people, and tongues, who stood before the throne and before the Lamb, clothed with white robes and palms in their hands, and cried with a loud voice, saying, Salvation to our God which sitteth upon the throne, and unto the Lamb." But when the *seventh and last seal* was opened, every tongue was mute—every soul was prostrate in the presence of the living God, and there was "silence in heaven about the space of half an hour." Rev. viii. 1. This state of mental silence, in which the active powers of man are all at rest and waiting upon God, was also prefigured in the institution of the Jewish or *Seventh-day* Sabbath, which the apostle Paul expressly says, was "a shadow of things to come." Col. ii. 17. And in another place, after speaking of the Seventh-day, he says, "There remaineth therefore a rest to the people of God; for he that hath entered into his rest, hath ceased from his own works as God did from his. Let us labour therefore to enter into that rest." Hebrews iv. 9–11.

They who have ceased from their own works, from the "will-worship and voluntary humility" of the natural man, are then prepared to enter into the closet of the heart, and shutting the door upon the world, to offer up their prayers in secret to the Father of spirits; and "he who seeth in secret, will reward them openly," by granting them ability to overcome every temptation that may assail them.

James. This doctrine would seem to exclude from public worship, not only instrumental music, but even the singing of hymns. Yet it appears to me, that there are directions somewhere in the new Testament for singing hymns and spiritual songs.

Father. Instrumental music is entirely without example or precept in the New Testament; and there is good reason to believe it never was used among Christians until the church became corrupted. It was much used in the worship of the Israelites under the old law, and was well suited to an outward, shadowy dispensation, when the Deity, in condescension to the ignorance and weakness of the people, was pleased to manifest himself in an outward temple made with hands. But we live under a spiritual dispensation, and are taught to believe, that " the Lord of heaven and earth dwelleth not in temples made with hands, neither is *worshipped with men's hands*, as though he needed any thing; seeing that he giveth to all life, and breath, and all things; that they should seek the Lord, if haply they might *feel after him and find him;* though he is not far from any one of us, for in him we live, and move, and have our being." Acts xvii. 24–28.

Music may have a tendency to allay the passions, and to quell for a moment the unsanctified desires of the human heart; but its influence is only temporary; for no sooner have its sounds ceased to vibrate on the ear, than the appetites and passions awake from their slumbers with unabated strength. Even the melody of David's harp, could only soothe for a while the evil spirit of Saul—it had no influence in changing his heart. The object of Christ's reign is not to send peace on earth, by *soothing the passions of men*, but a sword, to subdue them and bring them under right government. He comes to slay, that he may make alive again; to subjugate the will of man, in order that his divine will may be done in us, and to bring all our faculties, desires, and affections, under the government of his Holy Spirit. The pomp of ceremonies, the splendour of decorations, and the "pealing anthems" of the organ, are not consistent with the simplicity of spiritual worship, nor with the character and precepts of the meek and lowly Jesus.

It appears that the primitive Christians did sometimes sing psalms or spiritual songs, but the scriptures do not inform us whether it was always a part of their public worship, nor do they mention whether more than one person at a time was engaged in the service. It seems, from some expressions of the apostle Paul, that their mode of worship in the church at Corinth was different from any that now prevails in christendom. He says, " When you come together, *every one of you* hath a psalm, hath a doctrine, hath a tongue, hath a revelation, hath an interpretation. Let all things be done unto edifying.

If any man speak in an *unknown tongue*, let it be by two, or at most by three, and *that by course*, and let another interpret. But if there be no interpreter, let him keep silence in the church, and let him speak to himself and to God. Let the prophets speak two or three, and let the others judge. If any thing be revealed to another that sitteth by, let the first hold his peace; for ye *may all prophesy one by one*, that all may hear, and all may be comforted." 1 Cor. xiv. 26–31.

He also mentions singing, in two other of his epistles. He says, "Be not drunk with wine, wherein is excess, but be *filled with the Spirit*, speaking to yourselves in psalms, and hymns, and spiritual songs, making *melody in your hearts* unto the Lord." Eph. v. 18, 19. Again he says, " Let the *word of Christ* dwell in you richly in all wisdom; teaching and admonishing one another in psalms, and hymns, and spiritual songs; singing *with grace* in your hearts to the Lord." Col. iii. 16. In these passages it is observable that he is careful to mention that they must be filled with the spirit or word of Christ; and I think there is no doubt that their songs of praise and thanksgiving were dictated by it, just as much as their praying and prophesying. Every act of worship that proceeds from the influence of the Holy Spirit, is spiritual worship; and every act that proceeds from the *will and wisdom* of man, is "*will worship:*" the former is enjoined upon us; but the latter is expressly forbidden. Col. ii. 23.

We are recommended in the scriptures, not to neglect the assembling of ourselves together; and Christ has declared, "Where two or three are gathered together in my name, there am I in the midst of them." He also says, "Without me ye can do nothing." Now, does it not follow that when we are assembled together, we must wait in silence until we feel his power and presence to direct and assist us? For "*obedience* is better than sacrifice, and to *hearken*, than the fat of rams." They who act upon any other principle than this, appear to me to be like those who urged Jesus to go up to the feast: but he replied, "*My time is not yet come: your time is always ready.* The world cannot hate you, but me it hateth, because I testify of it that the works thereof are evil." John vii. 6, 7.

John. I should think it very uncharitable to say, that nearly all the worship that now prevails in Christendom is evil; for I am certain that there are many pious men in every Christian sect.

Father. I do not say their worship is evil; for I hope and believe much of it is accepted in the Divine sight. He who beholds the hearts of all men, has graciously promised, "To that man will I look, even to him that is poor and of *a contrite spirit,* and that trembleth at my word." There is a dead form of silence, as well as a dead form of words; and it is equally offensive in the Divine sight. They who merely sit in outward silence, pretending to present their bodies before the Lord, while their hearts are far from him, and their thoughts wandering in pursuit of earthly objects, are assembling in a dead form.

John. Is this dead form as dangerous as the other?

Father. In one respect I think it is not so dangerous; it does not encourage the practice of using improperly the words of holy men, and the promises of scripture. That which was true in the mouth of a saint, may be a falsehood in the mouth of a sinner.

James. Yes; I have often been struck with the impropriety of that practice, and I believe it not improbable, that many a well-meaning man utters more falsehoods in time of worship than in all the week besides.

Father. There are some hymns of such a general character, that almost any pious man may join in them without a breach of veracity; but it does not follow that they will always suit the state of his mind. There are other hymns and psalms which describe particular states of mind, and contain the expression of particular feelings and desires, which can only be sung with truth by those who are in the same state of mind. For instance, when David says, "As the hart panteth after the water-brooks, so panteth my soul after thee, O God. *My tears have been my meat* day and night, while they say unto me continually, Where is thy God?" Psalms xlii. 1, 3.

Now, how many singers are there in most congregations that can sing this psalm without departing from the truth? For those who are mourning, to sing the songs of joy, and for those who are rejoicing, to join the wail of sorrow, is equally inconsistent. He who joins a choir to sing in public, is expected to sing every thing that is selected for them; no matter how discordant his feelings may be, if his voice be harmonious, nothing more is required: and what is worse than all, persons who have musical talents are often induced to join the choir, while their hearts are unrenewed, and sometimes even while their moral characters are notoriously impure.

How offensive must it be to that omnipresent and holy Being, " who is of purer eyes than to behold iniquity," when he looks upon this solemn mockery, this approaching with the lips, while the heart is far from him! Will he not say to such persons, as he did to the Jews formerly, " Who has required this at your hands, to tread my courts? Bring no more vain oblations, incense is an abomination unto me, the new moons and sabbaths, the calling of assemblies I cannot away with; it is iniquity, even the solemn meeting." Under the old law, he who had touched a dead body, or an unclean beast, was not allowed to come into the congregation until he was purified; much less could he participate in an act of worship: and shall they who are " living in pleasures, and who are dead while they live," take an active part in public worship, under a more spiritual dispensation? It is evident that such cannot drink of the sup that Christ drank of, nor are they baptized with his baptism; and if they partake of the outward form while they deny and reject the life and substance, do they not drink unworthily to their own condemnation? These remarks will not apply to those sincere and pious worshippers who are really hungering and thirsting after righteousness; for unto them there always will be a blessing. But to this class I would seriously address the inquiry, whether that worship which is offered up in the will and wisdom of man, is not calculated to keep alive that will and to nourish that wisdom by which it is performed? Now we know that our wills must be subjected to the Divine will, and we are taught that "the wisdom of man is foolishness with God," when applied to spiritual things. "The kingdom of God is within you," says Christ; and it is altogether reasonable that he should be *known, and obeyed, and worshipped*, in his kingdom. If he veils his presence from us,—as he often does,—then we must wait upon him. "I wait for the Lord," says the psalmist, "*my soul doth wait—*my soul waiteth for the Lord, more than they that watch for the morning."—Ps. cxxx. 5, 6. The psalms of David, the writings of the prophets, the discourses of Jesus, and the epistles of Paul, contain a great many exhortations to *wait* upon the Lord, and *learn* *of him.* And John, the beloved apostle, writes to the Christians of his day, and tells them, "The *anointing* which ye have received of him *abideth* in you, and ye *need not that any man teach* you: but as the same anointing teacheth you of all things, and is truth and is no lie, and even as it hath taught you ye shall abide in him." 1 John ii. 27.

It is also said in many places in the scriptures, that Christ himself shall be the prophet, the leader, and the teacher of his people; for he alone is the true "shepherd and bishop of souls." Now while we have such exceeding great and precious promises, how unwise are they who "compass themselves about with sparks of their own kindling," instead of waiting in patience for the Divine influence to enable them to worship in spirit and in truth.

If Christ be the teacher of his people, they that would learn of him must sometimes learn in silence; for, if we are always thinking our own thoughts, and speaking our own words, or those of others, we cannot hear the instructions that are conveyed to the soul by the impressions of the Divine spirit.

If Christians of different denominations, cannot, at present, see the propriety of giving up their stated forms of prayer and praise, I am persuaded they would derive great advantage from appropriating *a part* of the time of their religious meetings to silent waiting upon God: it would give greater life and solemnity to the rest of their worship; and, independently of all other considerations, they would find it a most excellent discipline for the mind.

John. I find by experience, that when I wish to consider any thing attentively, I can do it best in silence; and it seems reasonable that our tongues should be still, when we undertake to examine our hearts.*

---

* A late writer, in speaking of what is termed "the Lord's Supper," makes this remark: "In all other instances of social worship, your attention is required without ceasing, to some *external* process, and you pass on from one part of the service to another with little opportunity to reflect as you proceed, or to pursue the suggestions which are made, in the manner that your own peculiar condition may require. But in this, the *leisure is given* for thoroughly applying to your own personal state, all that has met your ear, and for *pouring out freely the devotional feeling* which has been excited. And if there be any thing favorable to the soul, as multitudes of devout persons have insisted, in *occasions for contemplative worship in the presence of other men,* then in this respect the Lord's Supper may claim a superiority over every other sea-

Father. There is a very instructive fact mentioned in the history of the prophet Elijah, when he was in a cave on Mount Horeb. He was commanded to go forth and stand upon the mount before the Lord. "And behold the Lord passed by, and a great and strong wind rent the mountain, and brake in pieces the rocks before the Lord, but the Lord was not in the wind: and after the wind an earthquake, but the Lord was not in the earthquake: and after the earthquake a fire, but the Lord was not in the fire: and after the fire, a still small voice. And it was so when Elijah heard it, that he wrapped his face in his mantle and went out and stood in the entering in of the cave. And behold there came a voice unto him and said, What doest thou here, Elijah?" Thus it appears that Elijah knew that the word of the Lord (to which he had long been accustomed) was not to be heard in the noise and confusion of the outward elements,—but as soon as he heard the still small voice he wrapped his face in his mantle and listened to the Divine monitor. We have

---

son of social devotion." Now, if the pauses which occur during the administration of the Supper are found to be so salutary, why may they not be introduced at other times with equal advantage?

no reason to believe, that this "word of the Lord" which came to the prophets, was conveyed in sounds to the outward ear; for God is a spirit, and the soul of man is spiritual; therefore the word by which he speaks to the soul is also spiritual.

The apostle Paul writes to the Corinthians, saying, "Know ye not that ye are the temple of God, and that the spirit of God dwelleth in you? If any man defile the temple of God, him shall God destroy; for the temple of God is holy, which temple ye are." 1 Corinth. iii. 16, 17.

And the apostle Peter advises the Christians of his day, to "desire the sincere milk of the word, that," says he, "ye may grow thereby. If so be ye have tasted that the Lord is gracious. To whom coming as unto a living stone, disallowed indeed of men, but chosen of God and precious; ye also as lively stones are built up a *spiritual house*, a holy priesthood, to offer up spiritual sacrifices acceptable to God by Jesus Christ." 1 Peter ii. 3–6. Thus it appears that the soul of man is the temple of God, and that his church is a *spiritual house*, built up of living stones, of whom Jesus Christ is the "chief corner stone, elect and precious."

The temple of Solomon, with all its glory, was but a faint emblem or figure of this spiritual house which God is preparing for himself to dwell in, and in which he manifests his glory and his power.

It is written of Solomon's temple, that "it was built of stone *made* ready before it was brought thither: so that there *was neither hammer nor axe, nor any* tool of *iron, heard in the house* while it was in building." 1 Kings vi. 7. How striking a figure was this of the beautiful order and holy solemnity that ought to prevail, when *the living stones are brought together* in the assemblies of God's people! When we approach his awful presence to worship him in spirit and in truth, we should be careful not to employ the tools or ceremonies of man's invention; for the Lord, in directing his chosen people to build an altar, said, "An altar of earth shalt thou build unto me, and shalt sacrifice thereon thy burnt offerings and thy peace-offerings: and if thou wilt make me an altar of stone, thou shalt not build it of hewn stone: for if thou *lift up thy tool upon it, thou hast polluted it.*" Exodus xx. 24. Deut. xxvii. 5.

The offerings in God's temple are no longer of an outward nature, for "he is not worshipped with men's hands, as though he needed any thing." He requires us to give him the "first fruits" of all that we possess: we must serve him before all others, and give him the first place in our affections. The sacrifice which he accepteth is "a broken and a contrite spirit;" and the smoke of the incense which ascends up before him, is "the prayers of the saints." Rev. viii. 3.

I shall conclude this subject with a quotation from the writings of that great and good man, William Penn. "If," says he, "we are not to take thought what we shall say when we come before worldly princes, because it shall be given us, and that it is not we that speak, but the spirit of our Heavenly Father that speaketh in us; (Matt. x. 20,) much less can our ability be needed, or ought we to study to ourselves forms of speech in our approaches to the great Prince of princes, King of kings, and Lord of lords. The psalmist says, 'Lord, thou hast heard the desire of the humble, thou wilt prepare their heart, thou wilt cause thine ear to hear;' and says Wisdom, 'The preparation of the heart in man, and the answer of the tongue is from the Lord.' Here it is: thou must not think thy own thoughts, nor speak thy own words; which indeed is the silence of the holy cross; but be sequestered from all confused imaginations, that are apt to throng and press upon the mind in those holy retirements. It is not for thee to think to overcome the Almighty by the most composed matter cast into the aptest phrase:— no, no,—one groan, one sigh from a wounded soul; a heart touched with true remorse, a sincere and godly sorrow, which is the work of God's spirit, excels and prevails with God.— Wherefore, stand still in thy mind; wait to feel something that is divine to prepare and dispose thee to worship God truly and acceptably. And thus taking up the cross, and shutting the doors and windows of the soul against every thing that would interrupt this attendance upon God,— how pleasant soever the object be in itself,—how lawful and needful at another season,—the power of the Almighty will break in,—his spirit will work and prepare the heart, that it may offer up an acceptable sacrifice."

CONVERSATION III.

ON THE ORIGINAL AND PRESENT STATE OF MAN.

James. Brother John and I have lately been conversing about the original and present state of man, but we cannot agree in opinion, and have concluded to ask thy views upon the subject. He contends, that the transgression of Adam, in eating the forbidden fruit, produced an entire change in the nature of man, so that we are all born in a corrupt and sinful state; and that we are liable to punishment, not only for our own transgressions, but likewise on account of the guilt of our first parents, which he says is imputed to all their offspring. This doctrine I cannot believe; for it appears to me to be entirely inconsistent with the justice and mercy of the Divine Being, to impute to me a sin which I never committed; nor can I understand how the nature of man could be so completely changed by that one transgression of

Adam; for we do not find any *inherent* difference now between the children of the righteous and the children of the wicked; they appear to be all born in the same state, though it is acknowledged that the example and teaching of the parents have a great influence upon their characters.*

John. I do not reason in this way upon subjects of so momentous a character, but am content to refer to the scriptures of truth, which, being written by inspired men, are a much safer dependence than the fallible reason of man.

Father. I believe that all scripture, "given by inspiration of God, is profitable for doctrine, for reproof, for correction, for instruction in righteousness; that the man of God may be perfect, thoroughly furnished unto all good works." The truths contained in the scriptures, if properly understood and made the rule of our actions, are of inestimable value to man; but it is very evident that they cannot be understood without the exercise of reason; for a man de-

---

* The author does not deny that the dispositions and propensities of parents are often transmitted to their children, and that a race becomes degraded by a persistence in vice through several generations.

prived of reason could not derive the least benefit from them. They are addressed to the understandings of men; but owing to the imperfection of human language, they are liable to be misunderstood, especially by those who have no experimental knowledge of the things to which they relate. The most valuable parts of scripture are those which relate to spiritual things; but in order to understand them clearly, we must come to the knowledge of the things themselves. When we undertake to study any natural science, we are not satisfied with merely reading descriptions of natural objects, but we examine the objects for ourselves. For instance, the science of botany describes the various plants and flowers which the great Creator has so profusely scattered over the face of the earth; but we cannot obtain an accurate knowledge of them, merely by reading descriptions; we must ourselves examine the things described; and in order to do this, we must have *light to assist us*. Now this is the course we ought to pursue in the examination of spiritual things. The scriptures inform us, that "the kingdom of God is within us," and that it consists of "righteousness, peace, and joy in the Holy Spirit." But what will this description avail us, unless we look within us to find these things, and become obedient to the teachings of the Holy Spirit, whose light will make them manifest? There is much useful information in the scriptures, about the state of original purity in which man was created; the state of sin and corruption into which he has fallen by disobedience; and the state of restoration and salvation which is obtained by the faithful servants of Christ. This information is sometimes conveyed in plain and simple precepts, which may be understood literally; but it is often adorned with metaphors, and not unfrequently it is clothed in parables or allegories, according to the genius of the oriental languages. It is well known that Jesus frequently spake in parables, which were not generally understood by the multitude, and that he explained their meaning to his disciples. But even to his disciples he did not open every thing at once, for he said, "I have many things to say unto you, but ye cannot bear them now." There are many pious men, who do not doubt that the account given by Moses of the garden of Eden and the fall of our first parents, is literally true, yet they believe it has in it a spiritual signification of far more importance to us.

John. I am afraid to depend upon these spiritual significations, lest I should overlook the literal meaning of the text, and thus convert the whole Bible into an allegory. When any thing is stated as parable, I am then willing to look for a spiritual meaning, but not otherwise.

Father. It appears that the apostle Paul was of a different opinion; for he says, when speaking of the two sons which were born unto Abraham, that they were " an allegory" of " the two covenants." Gal. iv. 24. Yet Moses does not say it is an allegory, but relates it as a matter of history; and I have no doubt the facts did occur just as Moses has stated them, and that the spiritual meaning revealed to the apostle is *equally true.* It will be acknowledged by almost every experienced mind, that the account given by Moses of the journeying of the Israelites from Egypt through the wilderness to the promised land, contains a faithful and beautiful allegory of the Christian's progress from a state of darkness and sin, to a state of gospel light and salvation; yet who can suppose that this view of the subject impairs our belief of the facts related by Moses? With respect to the garden of Eden, in which man was originally placed when he was created, there can be no doubt that the account given by the inspired penman, is beautifully descriptive of that state of spiritual enjoyment which resulted to Adam from his dressing and keeping the trees of the garden; or, in other words, from his keeping in their proper order all the desires and affections of his animal and spiritual natures, which were given for the promotion of his happiness, and pronounced to be good. That the garden of Eden was considered among the holy men of old, as a state of spiritual enjoyment, we have an evidence in the writings of the prophet Ezekiel; for he says, in addressing the king of Tyrus, "Thus saith the Lord God, Thou sealest up the sum, full of wisdom and perfect in beauty. *Thou hast been in Eden, the garden of the Lord;* every precious stone was thy covering, the sardius, the topaz, and the diamond, the beryl, the onyx, the jasper, the sapphire, the emerald, the carbuncle, and gold; the workmanship of thy tabrets and thy pipes was *prepared in thee in the day that thou wast created.* Thou art the *anointed cherub* that covereth, and I have set thee so: thou wast upon *the holy mountain of God;* thou hast walked up and down in the midst of the stones of fire. Thou *wast perfect in thy ways from the day thou wast created,* till iniquity was found in thee." Ezek.

xxviii. 12 to 16. Behold, what a state of purity and wisdom was here, and that too "from the day he was created!" But he fell from this state of righteousness; for the prophet goes on to say, "By the multitude of thy merchandize they have filled the midst of thee with violence, and thou hast sinned. Therefore I will cast thee as profane out of the mountain of God; and I will destroy thee, O covering cherub, from the midst of the stones of fire!"

James. There is a very striking resemblance between the state here described, and that of our first parents as represented by Moses: for it appears that this king of Tyrus had "been in Eden, the garden of God;" that he was "full of wisdom and perfect in beauty;" and that he was "*perfect in his ways from the day he was created,* till iniquity was found in him." And it appears, too, that his punishment was similar to that of Adam; for he was "cast as profane out of the mountain of God." Now it becomes an interesting inquiry with me, whether the cause of his fall was not similar to that of Adam, and whether all men are not, like him, *created pure and innocent,* by the great Author of our being: for "have we not *all one Father?*" and "hath not one God created us?" Mal. ii. 10. And if

God is "the Father of spirits," as the apostle testifies, (Heb. xii. 9,) must not our souls come pure out of his hands?

Father. The first of these inquiries, in relation to the manner in which the king of Tyrus fell from his state of purity, is answered by the prophet Ezekiel. "Thus saith the Lord God, Because thy heart is lifted up, and thou hast said, I am a God; I sit in the seat of God, in the midst of the seas; yet thou art a man, and not God, though thou set thy heart as the heart of God." Now it appears that the sin of our first parents was somewhat analagous to this; for they were induced to believe that they "should be as Gods, knowing good and evil;" and after they had yielded to the temptation, "the Lord God said, Behold, the man is become as one of us, to know good and evil." Genesis iii. 5, 23.

James. There is a difficulty with me in understanding what Moses has said about the tree of the knowledge of good and evil, which was placed in the midst of the garden, and of which our first parents were forbidden to eat; for this appears to me like placing a temptation before them; and yet the apostle James has said,

God cannot be tempted with evil, *neither tempteth he any man."*

John. I cannot see that the difficulty would be removed, by saying that the tree here spoken of was some evil principle in the mind of Adam: for all his principles before the fall were derived from above. It appears to me that the temptation was suggested by the serpent, who was only an instrument of Satan, and endowed by him with a miraculous power of speech and reason. We are told that the evil one has the power of " transforming himself into an angel of light;" and therefore it was in his power to assume the form of a serpent, in order to effect his malicious designs.

James. As far as my own experience is concerned, I have no evidence of an evil spirit as existing separately from man; all my temptations have arisen from the perverted appetites and desires of my own nature, which are sometimes so disguised by self-love as to appear like ministers of happiness, or angels of light.

Father. I do not think we shall gain any thing by discussing the much-debated question about the existence of a devil: for, whether there be an evil spirit separate from man or not, I think it is very clear that unless our first parents had possessed in themselves a desire for the forbidden fruit, no persuasions of a disguised enemy could have induced them to eat it, contrary to the Divine prohibition. A person with no appetite for food, would never fall into the vice of gluttony, especially if he knew that it would destroy his life. It is said, "The woman saw that the tree was good for food, and that it was pleasant to the eyes, and a tree to *be desired to make one wise.*" Consequently she had an appetite or desire to partake of its fruit. This tree must have been created good, and intended for some good purpose; for when the work of creation was finished, "God saw every thing he had made, and behold it was very good." Now let us recur to our own experience, and we shall find that all our animal appetites, and all our mental desires and affections, are not only necessary to our existence, but conductive to our happiness, *when kept under the government of the Divine Spirit*, which gives life to the soul. It is only when they are *perverted from their original purpose* that they become instruments of evil. Adam was created in the image of God; that is to say, his mind was like the Divine mind, full of purity, benevolence, and joy; and he enjoyed the privilege of spiritual communion with God; which is to partake of "the tree of life, which is in the midst of the paradise of God." Rev. ii. 7. But, although he was made a free agent, he was not intended to be so independent of God as to know of himself what was good and what was evil, *without waiting for Divine direction.* And when he presumed to set up his own will, and to be governed by it in opposition to the Divine will, he *assumed the place of God;* and having thus turned away from the Holy Spirit, he ceased to partake of "the tree of life;" and, consequently, he died a spiritual death. It was thus that he experienced the fulfilment of the Divine prediction, "*In the day thou* eatest thereof, thou shalt surely die;" for, "*to be carnally minded is death;* but to be spiritually minded is life and peace." But in this state of alienation from God, Adam was not deserted by the mercy of his heavenly Parent; for he felt "the reproofs of instruction, which are the way of life." That same Divine Word which had been his joy and his consolation while in a state of innocence, now became his reprover and his chastener. It was to him as "a flaming sword, turning every way to keep the way of the tree of life," and to exclude him from the garden of Eden, which he was no longer worthy to enjoy. Every one who has attended to his own experience, knows what it is to be condemned for deviating from a known duty; how completely it shuts him out from a state of enjoyment, and prevents him from partaking of that peace of mind which is the reward of obedience. "For the word of God is quick and powerful, and sharper than any two-edged sword, piercing even to the dividing asunder of soul and spirit, and of the joints and marrow, and is a discerner of the thoughts and intents of the heart. Neither is there any creature that is not manifest in his sight; but all things are naked and open unto the eyes of him with whom we have to do." Heb. iv. 12. How merciful, how beneficent, is the Divine Author of our being, that he will not suffer us to rest in peace, while in a state of disobedience to his holy law! For in this state of alienation from him we never could be happy.

The happiness of man, both here and hereafter, is not made to depend upon any extraneous circumstances, such as the possession of an outward garden; but it depends upon the state of his mind, and the government of his affections. God is perfectly happy and beneficent himself, and he wills that all his creatures should be happy; but it is impossible for any to participate in his happiness, without becoming in some degree "partakers of his nature," and by the operations of the Holy Spirit, being renewed into the image of God, in which we were created.

John. This view of the subject is very different from the one I have always entertained, and it appears to me to be inconsistent with many passages in the scriptures of truth, as well as some facts in the present condition of man, which I shall endeavour to state. In the first place, man being created in the image of God, he must have been immortal; not subject to disease nor death, until he tasted the fruit of "that forbidden tree, whose mortal taste brought death into the world, with all our woe." But, having broken the Divine command, he incurred the penalty of death; which sentence was passed upon him when he was expelled from the garden, but the *execution* of the sentence was deferred for a long period; and he was doomed to eat his bread in the sweat of his face, till he returned unto the ground from whence he was taken.

Secondly. When Adam had eaten of this forbidden fruit, he lost the Divine image of holiness, wisdom, and immortality; and while in this state, his children were born unto him in his own image of fallen nature; consequently, they must have been born in a state of sin and subject to mortality.

Thirdly. There are many passages in the scriptures to confirm these views of the inherent depravity of man, through the sin of Adam. King David says, "I was shapen in iniquity, and in sin did my mother conceive me." And again, he says of the children of men, "They are all gone aside; they are altogether become filthy; there is none that doeth good, no not one." The apostle says, "We were by nature the children of wrath, even as others." It is also said in relation to the world before the flood, that "God saw that the wickedness of man was great in the earth, and that every imagination of the thoughts of his heart was only evil continually." That this state of depravity was owing to the sin of Adam, may be inferred from the writings of the apostle Paul; for he says, "As by one man sin entered into the world, and death by sin, and so death passed upon all men, for that all have sinned." Again he says, "As by one man's disobedience many were made sinners, so by the obedience of one shall many be made righteous:" for "as in Adam all die, even so in Christ shall all be made alive." That God does impute the sins of the parents to the children, may be proved from his dealings with the children of Israel; for he said he would "visit the sins of the fathers upon the children, to the third and fourth generation."

Lastly. I think these views are confirmed, by observing the actual condition of mankind in the world around us. See how much misery there is, resulting from depravity and sin; what raging passions desolate the moral world; what horrid crimes pollute the characters of men! Surely the destroyer has been here, and has left only a wreck behind, of all that was once so fair and beautiful. Nor is the corruption that reigns around us confined to the adult and the aged; even children seem to partake of it, and the first developments of character are marked with anger and impatience.

Father. I shall endeavour to answer these objections in the order in which they have been stated. And first: I agree that man, being in the Divine image, must have been immortal; but what part of him was made in the image of God? Surely it was not his earthly body; for "God is a Spirit," and " no man hath seen his shape at any time." I consider the body as the tabernacle or house in which the immortal soul dwells, during its state of probation, and I believe it was so considered by the inspired penmen; for Paul speaks of "our earthly house of this tabernacle being dissolved." 2 Cor. v. 1. To say that the *sentence* of death was passed upon Adam when he was driven from paradise, but the execution of the sentence was postponed for about *nine hundred* years, seems to me to be a very imperfect fulfilment of the Divine prediction, "In the day thou eatest thereof thou shalt surely die." Let us suppose that Adam and all his posterity had continued in the body until the present period, and that they had gone on to "multiply and replenish the earth," without any being removed by death; where would the countless myriads have found room for existence? I have no idea that the human body was ever intended to be immortal; for it was made of earthly materials, which are subject to decay; and we know that our bodies are continually changing by absorption and secretion, so that the particles which composed them at one period of life, are entirely removed at another. I do not think the mortality of our bodies is any proof of our being born in a state of sin;

for even the holy body of the Messiah was liable to death, or else he could not have been slain. He called his body his temple, saying, "Destroy this temple, and in three days I will raise it up." When I say that "the wages of sin is death" to the soul, I do not mean that the soul of the sinner ceases to exist, but that it ceases to be actuated by the Spirit of God, who is the life of the righteous soul: for it is said in the scriptures, that "they who are living in pleasures, are dead while they live." They have lost the influence of Divine life, and are like withered branches, ready to be cut off.

The second objection is founded on the children being born in the image of their parents. Now it is not said in Genesis, that Adam's children were all born in his image; for Seth is the only one mentioned as being born in his father's likeness. It is not an unusual thing, in the present day, for a child to bear the image of his father stamped on his person; but who among us would be so unjust as to impute to children the guilt of their parents, from a circumstance like this? It is said in the apocryphal book of the wisdom of Solomon, that by Divine Wisdom "the first formed father of the world was brought out of his fall;" and if any of his children were born after he was thus restored to the Divine image, can we suppose that these would be purer than the rest? I do not think they would, for we find no such effects in the present day.

I believe that every soul is the immediate gift and creation of God, agreeable to scripture testimony, "The dust shall return to the earth as it was, and the spirit shall return unto *God who gave it.*" Ecc. xii. 7. If therefore the soul or spirit of man be the gift of God, it must come pure out of his hands.

The third objection rests upon passages of scripture, all of which admit of a different interpretation, and one that is far more consistent with the character of a wise and benevolent Creator. A number of these passages speak in general terms of the whole human race, as being in a corrupt or fallen state, which I readily grant was true; but the scriptures themselves mention a number of exceptions. For instance, it is said of man before the flood, that "every imagination of the thoughts of his heart was only evil continually;" and that "God looked upon the earth, and behold it was corrupt; *for all flesh had corrupted his way upon the earth.*"— Yet it is said in the same chapter, that Noah, who was then living, was "*a just man, and perfect* in his generation," and that "*Noah walked with God.*"

It is very common, even now, to speak of cities and nations in general terms, and to give to a whole people the character which we think generally prevails among them; but no one supposes that, in such cases, there are not many exceptions. For my own part, I believe that there always have been good people in every age of the world, and that many who have passed through life unnoticed in the vale of obscurity, are now enjoying their reward in heaven. There are a great many excellent characters mentioned in the Bible, and some who are represented as *perfect*. "Enoch walked with God three hundred years, and he was not, for God took him." "Noah was a just man, and perfect in his generation." Job was "perfect and upright," and one that feared God and eschewed evil." It is said of Abraham, that he "obeyed the voice of God, and kept his commandments, and his statutes, and his laws." Gen. xxvi. 5. And he obtained the dignified title of "the friend of God." James ii. 23. The character of Joseph appears to have been without blemish, and it is said, "The Lord was with him." The prophet

Samuel was called in childhood to the service of God, and served him all his days.

It appears that there were good men in the days of king David, for he says, "Mark the *perfect man*, and behold *the upright*, for the end of that man is peace." There is reason to believe that Elijah was a perfect man, for he was translated; and Daniel, and some others of the prophets, appear to have lived in great favour with God. If such a state of perfection was attained by some before the Christian dispensation, may we not conclude that there have been a still greater number of such characters since?

There is not a single passage in the scriptures, which says that the guilt of Adam is imputed to his offspring;—they do not even prove that there is any *inherent* depravity in man. The expressions of David, where he says, "I was shapen in iniquity, and in sin did my mother conceive me," (Ps. li. 5,) were uttered at a time when he was under deep conviction for *actual transgression;* but if they must be taken literally, they only prove that his mother was a sinner.

What is sin? Is it not "the transgression of the law?" and "where there is no law, there is no transgression." Jesus said of the Jews, "If I had not come and spoken unto them, they had not had sin; but now they have no cloak for their sin." John xv. 22. The spirit of Christ still makes known to every man his duty; and until we disobey him, *we have no sin.* It is true that it is said, " By the disobedience of one man many have been made sinners;" but this expression may be applied to others besides Adam. It is said of Jeroboam the son of Nebat, that he "made Israel to sin;" and that "the children of Israel walked in all the sins of Jeroboam which he did; they departed not from them." Whereas it is said, that Josiah " made all that were present in Israel to serve the Lord their God; and all his days they departed not from following the Lord, the God of their fathers." Now, when we consider the relation in which Adam stood to the human family, it is not surprising that many of them should follow his early example; and that these again should influence others to swerve from the path of rectitude. Such a result is perfectly consistent with what we know of the character of man.

The apostle Paul, after speaking of "*the children of disobedience,*" (Eph. ii. 3,) says,

"Among whom we also had our conversation in times past, in the lusts of our flesh, *fulfilling the desires of the flesh and of the mind,* and were *by nature the children of wrath, even as others.*" But in another place, the same apostle says, "The Gentiles which have not the law, *do by nature the things contained in the law;* these having not the law, are a law unto themselves; which show forth the works of the law written in their hearts." Rom. ii. 14.

Now, if the first of these texts proves that some men have been sinners " by nature," the second one proves that others have been righteous " by nature." I understand the apostle's doctrine to be, that when we "*fulfil* the desires of the flesh and of the mind," we come into the nature of the children of wrath, who are the children of disobedience; but when we show forth the works of the Divine law written in our hearts, we become " partakers of the Divine nature." " As by one man sin entered into the world, and death by sin, and so death passed upon all men, *for that all have sinned.*" Here the reason is assigned why spiritual death hath passed upon all men; it is *because all have sinned*, and not because of any imputed guilt. And the same apostle has said, that " as in

Adam all die, even so in Christ shall all be made alive." He does not say that we all died in Adam; but he speaks in the *present tense*, and says, "In Adam all die." Now let us consider what nature it is that we have derived from Adam. Is it not our animal nature? It cannot be our spiritual nature; for God only is "the Father of spirits." Heb. xii. 9. If, then, we are governed by this animal or earthly nature which we derive from Adam, we die; for "to be carnally minded is death;" but if we become obedient to "the law of the spirit of life in Christ Jesus," we shall live; for to "be spiritually minded is life and peace." The name Adam, signifies earthy; and the apostle says, "The first man is of the earth, earthy." The first developments which take place in the infancy of man, are his animal appetites; for, "that is not first which is spiritual, but that which is natural, and afterwards that which is spiritual." These appetites are necessary to our animal existence, and they are not evil in themselves; but they become evil to us, when we suffer them to have dominion over us, for they are good servants, but bad masters.

It is abundantly evident, from the convictions of our own minds, as well as from the scriptures, that God does not impute to us any sins but those which we have ourselves committed; for who has ever felt any compunction for the sins of his ancestors? If, therefore, our heart condemn us not, then have we confidence towards God." 1 John iii. 21. It is true, that God said to the children of Israel, "I the Lord thy God am a jealous God, visiting the iniquities of the fathers upon the children unto the third and fourth generation;" but observe, he adds, "*of them that hate me.*" Ex. xx. 5. It is evident, however, that we do feel the natural effects of our father's conduct, whether it be good or whether it be evil. He whose life is regulated by the principles of pure religion, endeavours to bring up his children in the way they should go, and when he is gone, they will feel the good effects of his virtuous example and unsullied reputation. But, on the contrary, the wicked man often subjects his children to misery and disgrace even to the third and fourth generation. How awful, then, is the responsibility of parents! How should these considerations incite us to diligence and watchfulness, lest it be said to us in the day of solemn reckoning, "Where are the lambs I committed to thy charge?"

So far is the doctrine of original sin from being taught in the Bible, that there are several passages directly against it. One of the most striking of these is in the book of the prophet Ezekiel, who was sent to the children of Israel, expressly to reprove them for having taught this doctrine. He says: "What mean ye that ye use this proverb concerning the land of Israel, saying, The fathers have eaten sour grapes, and the children's teeth are set on edge? As I live, saith the Lord, ye shall not have occasion any more to use this proverb in Israel. Behold *all souls are mine;* as the soul of the *father,* so *also the soul* of the son is mine: the *soul that sinneth, it shall die."*—xviii. 2–4. "Yet, say ye, why? doth not the son bear the iniquity of the father? When the son hath done that which is lawful and right, and hath kept all my statutes and done them, he shall surely live. The *soul that sinneth, it shall die.* The *son shall not bear the iniquity of the father,* neither shall the father bear the iniquity of the son: the righteousness of the righteous shall be upon him, and the wickedness of the wicked shall be upon him. But if the wicked will turn from all his sins that he hath committed, and keep all my statutes, and do that which is lawful and right, he shall surely live, he shall not die. All his transgressions that he hath committed, *they shall not be mentioned unto him: in his righteousness that he hath done he shall live.* Have I any pleasure at all that the wicked should die? saith the Lord God: and not that he should return from his ways and live?" verses 19–23. "Yet ye say, the way of the Lord is not equal. Hear now, O house of Israel! Is not my way equal? Are not your ways unequal?" v. 25.

This language appears to me as strong as it could be against the doctrine of original sin.— The language of Jesus Christ is also conclusive on this point. He says, "Suffer little children, and forbid them not, to come unto me; for of such is the kingdom of heaven." "Verily, I say unto you, except ye be converted, and become as little children, ye shall not enter into the kingdom of heaven." Matt. xviii. 3, and xix. 14. Now it is evident from this, that little children must be born in a state of purity; for no unclean thing can enter into the kingdom of God.

I shall now proceed to consider the fourth and last objection, which relates to the present condition of man as displayed in the world around us. And I must acknowledge that a large proportion of mankind appear to be so far alienated from the Divine harmony, that we may consider them in a fallen state; but this fact being admitted, it does not follow, as a necessary consequence, that they were *born* in a state of impurity and sin; it only shows that all are born with appetites and propensities, which, if *improperly indulged*, will lead to sin; and Adam himself must have been created with similar appetites, or else he never would have fallen. Let us examine some of these appetites and desires, and I think we shall find them wisely adapted to the condition of man.

The first appetite that we discover in infancy, is hunger, which prompts the child to partake of food, before it can reason upon its use; and if its food is withheld, it is prompted to cry for it, so as to excite the compassion of its parents, but it is not in childhood only that this appetite is subservient to our welfare. How many there are who would neglect the proper nourishment of their bodies, if they were not impelled to it by the cravings of hunger, and by the hope of that pleasurable sensation which is derived from partaking of food? Yet the desire for food, thus produced in man, will, if *improperly indulged*, lead to the vice of gluttony. Nearly the same observations will apply to the appetite of thirst, and the pleasure that attends its gratification: yet the inordinate indulgence of this appetite leads to the dreadful vice of intemperance, which has wrought such misery and desolation in the human family. The desire for rest is also necessary for recruiting our bodily strength, and its gratification is attended with a sensible pleasure; but its improper indulgence leads to indolence, disease, and depravity. The desire for action is one of our natural propensities that is very conspicuous in childhood, and its exercise is conductive to the health of both body and mind. It is this that often impels to useful labour, and renders even labour a pleasure. But how many evils arise from the desire of employment, when it takes a wrong direction? Thus, the vice of gambling is one among the many expedients that have been invented "to kill time," and to fill up those vacant hours which ought to be devoted to nobler purposes. The desire for knowledge is one of the noblest impulses of the mind, and the exercise of it is accompanied by an exalted pleasure: yet this desire, when directed to frivolous or useless objects, degenerates into a vain curiosity, which is productive of evil.

Thus we might proceed to examine all the desires and affections of our animal and spiritual natures, and we should find them all to be the good gifts of a gracious God, and " trees of his right-hand planting :" but, like the elements of the natural world, they are all liable to abuse. Thus, conjugal and parental love are good in themselves, but they may degenerate into idolatry. Emulation may lead to envy; and the desire for power may end in avarice or ambition.

It has pleased the benevolent Author of our being to attach a peculiar pleasure to the gratification of these desires, when they are kept *within their proper bounds:* but no sooner do we indulge them beyond this point, than they become the instruments of our chastisement.— Even that natural feeling of displeasure or aversion, which is occasioned by a positive injury inflicted upon ourselves or upon others, if it be permitted to arise to anger, will give us pain. Yet I believe it is a good principle, when directed only against the *wickedness of men*, without being accompanied by any ill-will towards them; for the Divine Being himself condemns " all unrighteousners," at the same time that he is " kind even to the unthankful and to the evil."

How beautiful—how perfectly adapted to our wants, is the original constitution of man! especially when we take into view that Divine principle of light which shines in the soul, and enables us to perceive what is our duty towards God and our fellow-men; which is comprehended in "doing justly, loving mercy, and walking humbly with God!" Mic. vi. 8. The virtuous affections have been likened to the gales which waft the vessel on her way, and this Divine monitor is the pilot who sits at the helm and guides her to the destined port. How much it is to be lamented that the free teachings of this Divine principle are neglected, while so many are looking outward to men and to books for instruction, instead of looking within themselves for the kingdom of heaven, which consists in "righteousness, peace, and joy in the Holy Spirit!"

John. I remember in our last conversation thou told us that man has "nothing good in himself." Does not that sentiment conflict with some of the views thou hast just expressed?

Father. I said he had nothing good in himself independent of the Divine Being; which does not conflict with my present views; for "there is but one that is good, that is God." However noble may be the faculties he has given to man, they cease to be good as soon as they cease to be governed by him. God is the sun and centre of his spiritual creation; and as soon as we depart from under the restraining influence of his love, we fall into a state of disorder and confusion. But he desires that we should serve him from choice, and not from compulsion; and therefore, while he has bound the material universe in chains, he has "left free the human will."

All the dealings of God towards his creatures are founded in eternal love: even the sufferings which result from the abuse of his gifts, seem intended to bring back the delinquents to the path of rectitude, which is the only state where happiness can be attained. His commands and his prohibitions are all for our good, and are wisely designed for the promotion of our present and eternal welfare. It is a law which he has stamped upon our nature, that virtue will always produce happiness, and vice will always bring misery: they do so now, and they must continue to do so forever. How important then it is, that we should cultivate those benevolent affections which are calculated to bring us into the image of God; for, as we become "partakers of his nature," we shall participate in his happiness; and when we leave this scene of probation, we shall be fitted to enter into those spiritual joys which are prepared for the righteous.

How ardently do I desire that all my fellow-creatures may become sensible of the true dignity of man! which does not depend on the abundance of riches, nor on the attainments of learning, nor on the possession of intellectual power; but it consists in being made "partakers of the Divine nature," enjoying communion with the Holy Spirit, and becoming "heirs of God, and joint heirs with Christ."

CONVERSATION IV.

ON THE DIVINE BEING.

James. Since our last interview, brother John and I have been conversing on the attributes of the Divine Being, and his manifestations to the children of men in different ages of the world. He appears to think there is something so mysterious in the subject, that we ought to believe without understanding it: but I am opposed to every thing like implicit belief: and as different doctrines are taught among men, I cannot believe any of them, until the subject shall become clear to my own understanding.

John. Here is the difference between brother James and myself: he is determined to measure every thing by his own finite understanding, even the three-fold existence of the infinite God; but I do not feel at liberty to doubt any thing that appears to be clearly recorded in the holy scriptures, although it may be beyond my limted comprehension: for I find, that even in the works of creation, there are many things that I do not understand, yet it is impossible to doubt them. For instance, I know there is an intimate connection between the soul and the body, and yet I cannot understand how they are united, nor how a material body can be acted on by an immaterial soul. We cannot understand *how* the simplest operations in nature take place. For example, the growth of grass is a fact that we all acknowledge, but we do not understand how it takes place. I therefore conclude, that it would be a piece of great folly in me to attempt to understand the mystery of three persons in the Godhead; for if the scriptures assure us of the fact, I ask no further evidence.

Father. I am willing to explain to you my views upon the subject, and I wish you to state all the objections that may occur to you; for it is my desire that we may all be seekers of truth, and not the champions of a party. Before I proceed to state my views upon the main question, I must make a few remarks upon the subject of belief.

It appears to me, that belief does not depend entirely upon our own will; for we often hear things asserted, that we could not believe if we

ON THE DIVINE BEING. 113

were to try. If a man who was really very sick, were told by his physician that he was not sick, and that he might get up and walk, it is very certain that the sick man would not believe him, although he might wish it were in his power to believe.

Belief depends upon the weight of evidence presented before the mind, and upon our having a *clear perception* of that evidence. If the mind be clouded by the prejudices of education, or biased by interest, it will not always *perceive* the evidence *on both sides*, that may be presented to it; which is a fact that may be illustrated by our outward vision: for when a great number of objects are presented before us at the same time, the eye will naturally rest upon those objects which are *most agreeable to us*, and will sometimes overlook other objects, so as not to perceive them at all. We therefore make up our opinions according to the evidence that *we perceive;* and if we perceive only a part of the evidence, we may be *irresistibly* led to form an erroneous opinion. But if, at any time afterwards, we come to *perceive* the *remaining* evidence, we shall then be obliged to change this opinion. Therefore, I do not condemn any man for entertaining opinions different from my own;

for I conclude that one or the other of us has not seen the subject in all its bearings; and I feel assured, that if we are both faithful to *put in practice* all that we do *know to be good*, the Divine Being will not leave us without sufficient light to guide our steps in the way that leads to eternal peace.

There are many facts which we cannot explain, and yet we are obliged to believe them, because the evidence of their existence is so plain as to leave no room for doubt. In this case, it is *the fact* that is the object of our belief, and not the *manner* or *process* by which the fact has been produced; for if this *process* be hidden from us, it *cannot be an object of belief.* For instance, in the cases mentioned by John; the union of the soul and body, and the action of the soul upon the body, *are facts* which I cannot doubt; but *the manner* in which they are united, and the *principle* by which the soul acts upon the body, are hidden from me, and consequently *this manner* and *this principle* are not the objects of my belief. That the grass grows is *a fact* for which I have the evidence of my senses; but so far as I cannot perceive the *process* by which it grows, this process is not an object of my belief. The human mind is sc constituted that we cannot believe without sufficient evidence; nor can we believe any proposition that contains in itself a contradiction or an absurdity: for no evidence can prove a thing that contradicts itself. For instance, if a person were to say that a part of any given thing is as large as the whole of it: here is a contradiction that no authority whatever could make me believe. Compulsion may make hypocrites, but it never can make believers. It is related of Socrates, that when he was asked his opinion of some writings that were very obscure, he replied that he approved of those parts which he understood, and he therefore concluded that the parts which he did not understand were equally good. This is the conclusion I have formed with regard to the scriptures; and therefore I am far from rejecting any passage which I do not understand; for I apprehend there may be truths contained in such passages, which, in a more advanced stage of experience, will become clear to my mind.

James. This explanation is satisfactory to me: but I believe it is very common for men to withdraw their attention from that kind of evidence which does not accord with their *prejudices* and *passions;* and this is a species of wilful neglect, for which we shall certainly be held accountable. The term mystery, which is so often used by religious teachers in order to extricate themselves from the absurdities of their own doctrines, has been perverted from its original meaning. A *mystery*, among the ancients, was not a doctrine supposed to be incomprehensible in itself; but it was something that was hidden, or withheld from the public, and only revealed to a favoured few; and therefore, when it was revealed to any one, it was no longer a mystery to him.

Father. There are two kinds of mysteries mentioned in the scriptures. The first is that kind to which Christ alludes, when he says to his disciples, "It is given to you to know the mysteries of the kingdom of heaven, but to them it is not given." Matt. xiii. 11. These mysteries are not revealed through the wisdom or learning of man; for he says, "I thank thee, O Father, Lord of heaven and earth, that thou hast hid these things from the wise and prudent, and hast revealed them unto babes: even so, Father, for so it seemed good in thy sight."— Luke x. 21. "Even *the mystery*," says the apostle, "which hath been hid from ages and from generations, but now is made manifest to his saints; to whom God would make known what is the riches of the glory of this *mystery among the Gentiles;* which is, Christ in you, the hope of glory." Col. i. 26, 27.

From these passages, it appears, that the mysteries of the kingdom of God are only revealed to the children of the kingdom, who are the meek, the humble, the teachable, as babes; and they are hidden from the wise and prudent of this world; that is, from those who attempt to understand them by the wisdom and learning of man, without coming to the experimental knowledge of the truth. There is, however, another kind of mystery, called the "*mystery of iniquity,*" which the apostle Paul said had begun to work, even in his day, and should be more fully revealed in " the man of sin and son of perdition," who " opposes and exalts himself above all that is called God, or that is worshipped; so that he as God sitteth in the temple of God, showing himself that he is God."— 2 Thess. ii. 3–7. This is the same kind of mystery which the apostle John alludes to in the Revelations; for he describes the apostate church as "a woman sitting upon a scarlet-colored beast, full of names of blasphemy; and upon her forehead was a name written, *Mystery,*

Babylon, the great." It appears that the apostle Paul forewarned the church of Colosse against the particular snare that would cause this "falling away;" for he says, "As ye have therefore received Christ Jesus the Lord, so walk ye in him, rooted and built up in him, and stablished in the faith, as ye have been taught, abounding therein with thanksgiving. Beware lest any man spoil you through *philosophy and vain deceit,* after *the traditions of men,* after *the rudiments of the world,* and not after Christ; for in him dwelleth all the fulness of the Godhead bodily." Col. ii. 6–9.

Let us now turn our attention to the history of the Christian church, and trace the progress of this "mystery of iniquity," until it became inscribed on the very front of her doctrines. In order to show this, I will quote a few sentences from Mosheim's Ecclesiastical History. In his account of the *first century,* he says:—
"The method of teaching the sacred doctrines of religion, was at *this time* most simple, far removed from all the subtle rules of philosophy, and all the precepts of human art. This appears abundantly, not only in the writings of the apostles, but also in all those of the second century which have survived the ruins of time.

Neither did the apostles, or their disciples, ever think of collecting into a regular system the principal doctrines of the Christian religion, or of demonstrating them in a scientific and geometrical order. The beautiful and candid simplicity of those early ages, rendered such philosophical niceties unnecessary; and the great study of those who embraced the gospel, was, rather to express its divine influence in their *dispositions* and *actions*, than to examine its doctrines with an excessive curiosity, or to explain them by the rules of human wisdom.— There is indeed extant, a brief summary of the principal doctrines of Christianity in that form, which bears the name of the apostles' creed, and which, from the *fourth century* downwards, was almost generally considered a production of the apostles. All, however, who have the least knowledge of antiquity, look upon this *opinion as entirely false*, and destitute of all foundation." *
In treating of the second century, he says, " This venerable simplicity was not indeed of a long duration; its beauty was gradually *effaced by the laborious efforts of human learning*, and the dark subtleties of imaginary science. Acute

---

* Ecc. His. London ed. 1826, p. 84.

researches were employed upon several religious subjects, concerning which ingenious decisions were pronounced; and, what was worst of all, several tenets of a chimerical philosophy were imprudently incorporated into the Christian system "*

In reviewing the doctrines of the third century, he says: " But the *Christian doctors* who had applied themselves to the *study of letters and philosophy*, soon abandoned the frequented paths, and struck out into the devious wilds of fancy. The Egyptians distinguished themselves in this new method of explaining the truth."† But when he comes to the fourth century, he says, " The fundamental principles of the Christian doctrine were preserved *hitherto* uncorrupted and entire in most churches, though it must be confessed, that they were often explained and defended in a manner that discovered the greatest ignorance and utter confusion of ideas. The disputes carried on in the Council of Nice concerning the *three persons in the Godhead*, afford a remarkable example of this, particulary in the language and explanations of those *who approved of the decisions of that council.* So little light,

---

* Ecc. His. London ed. 1826, p. 135.   † *Ibid.* p. 200.

precision, and order, reigned in their discourses, that they appear to substitute three Gods instead of one "* Again, he says: " The faction of the Donatists was not the only one that troubled the church during *this century. Soon after its commencement,* even in the year 317, a new contention *arose in Egypt,* upon a subject of much higher importance, and with consequences of a yet more pernicious nature. The subject of this fatal controversy, which kindled such deplorable divisions throughout the Christian world, was the doctrine of *three persons in the Godhead;* a doctrine which, in the *three preceding* centuries, had happily *escaped the vain curiosity of human researches,* and been left undefined and undetermined by any particular set of ideas."† The emperor Constantine assembled, in the year 325, the famous council at Nice, in Bythinia, wherein the deputies of the church universal were summoned to put an end to this controversy. In this council, " after many keen debates and violent efforts of the two parties, the doctrine of Arius was condemned; Christ declared consubstantial, or of the same essence with the Father; the vanquished pres-

---

* Ecc. His. London ed. 1826, p. 269.   † *Ibid.* p. 302.

byter *banished among the Illyrians*, and his followers *compelled to give their assent to the creed or confession* of faith which was composed by this council."*

Thus was established by law, for the first time, the doctrine of the trinity; which, it does not appear, was ever heard of till nearly three hundred years after the promulgation of Christianity. This doctrine seems to have originated in the speculations of visionary philosophers,—it was established by a council of contentious bishops,—and enforced by the sword of a Roman emperor. Previous to this time, different opinions had been entertained on this subject, "without giving the least offence;"† but now "the woman" was seated on the beast of temporal power; the name of "*mystery*" was written on her forehead; and she went on *from this period*, multiplying her absurd doctrines and ridiculous ceremonies, and persecuting all who would not conform to them; until at length she became "drunken with the blood of the saints, and with the blood of the martyrs of Jesus."

James. This piece of history is very instruct-

---

* Ecc. His. London ed. 1826, p. 305.   † *Ibid.* p. 303.

ive; it shows us how very dangerous it is to give up our own understandings, and to receive without examination whatever doctrines may be taught by the ministers of religion. Every *practical Christian* who reads his Bible and examines the book of his own experience, is just as capable of judging for himself as the most learned priest or professor of theology. It appears that the scholastic divines of the fourth century not only forced a creed upon the people, but many of the bishops had the address to obtain large revenues * for teaching these mysteries, which they did not themselves understand. If people can only be persuaded to shut their eyes, they may be led any where; for then they can no longer distinguish between darkness and light.

John. It appears to me, that the doctrine of the trinity is taught in the scriptures, although the *name* is not found there. I cannot see how any person who believes in the divinity of Christ can doubt this doctrine; for if we believe that the Father, Son, and Holy Ghost, are each of them Divine, it appears to me that the doctrine is established,—unless we say that these are

---

* Mosheim, p. 195.

only three different names for one and the same Being.

Father. I believe in the divinity of Christ, but I cannot receive the doctrine of three persons in one God. The views of William Penn on this subject are so consistent with my own, and so well expressed, that I will quote them to you. He says, "I sincerely own, and unfeignedly believe in ONE, holy, just, merciful, almighty, and eternal God, who is the father of all things; that appeared to the holy patriarchs and prophets of old, at sundry times and in divers manners; and in one Lord Jesus Christ, the everlasting wisdom, divine power, true light, only Saviour and preserver of all, *the same ONE, holy*, just, merciful, almighty, and *eternal God*, who in the fulness of time took and was manifested in the flesh; at which time he preached (and his disciples after him) the everlasting gospel of repentance, and promise of remission of sins and eternal life to all that heard and obeyed; who said, He that is with you, (in the flesh,) shall be in you, (by the spirit,) and though he left them, (as to the flesh,) yet not comfortless, for he would come to them again, (in the spirit;) for a little time they should not see him, (as to the flesh,) again a little while and they should see him (in the spirit;) for the Lord (Jesus Christ) is that Spirit, a manifestation whereof is given to every man to profit withal. In which Holy Spirit I believe as the *same almighty and eternal God;* who, as in those times he ended all shadows, and became the infallible guide to them that walked therein, by which they were adopted heirs and co-heirs of glory; so am I a living witness that the same holy, just, merciful, almighty, and eternal God, is now, as then, (after this tedious night of idolatry, superstition, and human inventions, that hath overspread the world,) gloriously manifested, to save from all iniquity, and to conduct into the holy land of pure and endless peace; in a word, to tabernacle in men." *—[See Penn's Innocency with her open face.]

John. Although I acknowledge that William Penn was a great and good man, I cannot take his expressions as sufficient authority; I look to a higher source, even to the scriptures of truth, for evidence on this important question. Now,

---

* See 1 Cor. viii. 5, 6; Heb. i. 1; 1 Cor. viii. 6; John i. 14; 1 Tim. iii. 16; Matt. iv. 17; Luke xxiv. 47; John xiv. 17, 18, xvi. 16; 2 Cor. iii. 17; 1 Cor. i. 7; Romans viii. 14, 17; Rev. xxi. 3; Proverbs xxviii. 13.

the scriptures appear to me to speak of the Deity in a threefold sense :—first, as the Creator and Father of all; secondly, as the Son, who is the mediator between God and man; and thirdly, as the Holy Ghost, who is sent by the Father and·the Son, to sanctify the heart and regulate the affections. Yet it is repeatedly said in the Old and New Testament, that God is one; therefore, we conclude that there are three persons in one God,—each of which persons is perfect in himself, possessing omnipotence, omniscience, and eternity; the "same in substance, equal in power, eternity, and glory." [See Westminster Confession.] I shall now endeavor to prove these positions by passages from scripture.

1st. That there is *more than one* person in the Godhead, may be inferred from the following texts: "God said, let *us* make man in *our* image, after *our* likeness." Gen. i. 26. "And the Lord God said, the man has become as one of *us*, to know good and evil." Gen. iii. 26. And the prophet says, "I heard the voice of the Lord, saying, whom shall I send, and who shall go for *us?*" Isaiah vi. 8. We are also informed by learned men, that the name most commonly given to the Deity, in the Old Testament, is Elohim, which is a plural noun; and this has been considered a strong proof that there is a plurality of persons in the Godhead.

2d. That the number of persons in the Deity is three, may be concluded from the words of our Lord, who said to his disciples, "Go ye, therefore, and teach all nations, baptizing them in the name of the Father, and of the Son, and of the Holy Ghost." Matt. xxviii. 19. And also from the benediction of the apostle Paul, who says, "The grace of our Lord Jesus Christ, and the love of God, and the communion of the Holy Ghost, be with you all." 1 Corinth. xiii. 14.

3d. We argue that each of these is, in some sense distinct, because one is represented as the Father, who sends; another as the Son, who is sent into the world; and the third as the Spirit, that was poured out upon all flesh. The Father and Son are also represented, in many places, as speaking to each other, which shows that they must be distinct from each other in one sense, although forever united in another. Now, I think it may be proved that each of these persons is Divine, and consequently co-eternal and co-equal. That the Father is omnipotent, omniscient, and eternal, will, I suppose, be admitted without argument. That the Son is so, may be shown from the introduction to the Gospel by St. John. "In the beginning was the Word, and the Word was with God, and the Word was God. The same was in the beginning with God. All things were made by him, and without him was not any thing made that was made." Ch. i. 2. "And the Word was made flesh and dwelt among us, (and we beheld his glory, the glory as of the only begotten of the Father,) full of grace and truth."—verse 14. There are many other texts of similar import, but I shall quote only one more, which I consider sufficient. St. Paul says, "God, who at sundry times, and in divers manners, spake in time past unto the fathers by the prophets, hath in these last days spoken unto us by his Son, whom he hath appointed heir of all things, by whom also he made the worlds; who being the brightness of his glory, and the express image of his person, and upholding all things by the word of his power, when he had by himself purged our sins, sat down on the right hand of the Majesty on high." Heb. i. 1–3.

That the Holy Ghost is not only Divine, but personally distinct from the others, may be inferred from the operations assigned to them being generally different. He is represented as the baptizing power; Christians are also said to be born of the Spirit: and Christ promised his disciples, "I will pray the Father, and he shall give you *another Comforter*, that he may abide with you for ever, even the Spirit of truth."—John xiv. 16.

4th. Having now shown from scripture that there are three persons in the Deity, it only remains to be proved that Jesus Christ is the second person, or Logos, mysteriously united to "a human body and rational soul," and born of a virgin; and this has been called the hypostatical union. This may be proved from many passages. It is said, "He *took* not on him the nature of angels, but he took on him the seed of Abraham; wherefore, in all things it behoved him to be made like unto his brethren, that he might be a merciful and faithful highpriest, in things pertaining to God, to make reconciliation for the sins of the people; for in that he himself hath suffered, being tempted, he is able to succour them that are tempted."—Heb. ii. 16–18. He is also called "God manifest in the flesh." 1 Tim. iii. 16. "God with us." "The Lord of glory." 1 Cor. iii. 8. And, "over all, God blessed for ever." Rom. ix. 5. That he had a human soul, as well as a human body, is very clear; for he says, "My soul is exceeding sorrowful, even unto death." Yet his human nature must not be confounded with his divine; for, though there be an union of natures in Christ, yet there is not a mixture or confusion of them or their properties. His humanity is not changed into his Deity; nor his Deity into his humanity; but the two natures are *distinct in one person*. How this union exists is above our comprehension; and indeed, if we cannot explain how our bodies and souls are united, it is not to be supposed we can explain this astonishing mystery of "God manifest in the flesh." [See Buck's Theo. Dict. article Jesus Christ — also, Smith's Treatise on the Trinity.]

Father. Those who profess to derive their doctrines entirely from the scriptures, ought to be very careful to keep the language of scripture, especially when speaking on a subject that they do not pretend to understand. If the doctrine of a trinity be taught in the scriptures, it must be conveyed by inspiration in the very best language which could be chosen; and there is no need of *inventing new terms* to express it. But we do not find any such term in the scriptures as a trinity, nor is it said that there are three persons in the Godhead; nor is there any language there conveying the same ideas. I therefore conclude, that this doctrine is an invention of men; and it must be acknowledged by every reader of history, that it has been one of the principal causes of dissention and persecution ever since it was introduced into the church. If we take the word *person* in its common acceptation, it means an individual, or a being; and if we say there are three infinite persons in one Being, *each* of whom has *all power* and *all wisdom*, the proposition contains in itself a contradiction that is obvious to the meanest capacity. Therefore the advocates of this doctrine are obliged to admit that the term *person* does not exactly convey their meaning, and that they only use it for want of a better. Why then should they contend so strenuously for words that do not convey their meaning?

I shall now proceed to examine the foundation on which this doctrine rests.

In the first place,—It is said that the use of the plural pronouns *us* and *our*, ascribed to the Divine Being, and the circumstance of one of the names given to him in the scriptures being a *plural noun*, indicate that there is more than one person in the Deity. This peculiarity in the Hebrew language* has furnished one of

---

* The late learned and amiable Hindoo reformer, Rammohun Roy, remarks: "Were we even to disregard totally the idiom of the Hebrew, Arabic, and of almost all Asiatic languages, in which the plural number is often used for the singular to express the respect due to the person denoted by the noun; and to understand the term 'our image' and 'our likeness,' found in the verse, [Gen. i. 26] as conveying a plural meaning, the quotation would still by no means answer their purpose: for the verse in question would in that case imply a plurality of Gods, without determining whether their number was three or three hundred, and of course without specifying their persons. No middle point in the unlimited series of number being determined, it would be almost necessary, for the purpose of obtaining some fixed number, as implied by those terms, to adopt either two, the lowest degree of plurality in the first personal pronoun both in Hebrew and Arabic, or to take the highest number of Gods with which human imagination has peopled the heavens. In the former case, the verse cited might countenance the doctrine of the duality of the Godhead, entertained by Zirdusht and his followers, representing the God of goodness and the God of evil, to have jointly created man, composed of a mixed nature of good and evil propensities: in the latter, it would be consistent with the Hindoo system of religion: but there is nothing in the words, that can be with any the strong arguments of trinitarians; but they appear to forget that the same kind of plural

---

justice construed as pointing to Trinity. These are not the only difficulties attending the interpretation of those terms:—if they should be viewed in any other than a singular sense, they would involve contradiction with the very next verse: 'So God created man in his own image;' in which the singular number is distinctly used: as in Deut. ch. iv. ver. 4: 'The Lord our God is one Lord;' and also with the spirit of the whole of the Old Testament.

"To those who are tolerably versed in Hebrew and Arabic, (which is only a refined Hebrew,) it is a well-known fact, that in the Jewish and Mohummudan scriptures, as well as in common discourse, *the plural form is often used in a singular sense*, when the superiority of the subject of discourse is intended to be kept in view. This is sufficiently apparent from the following quotations, taken both from the Old Testament in Hebrew, and from the Qoran. Exo. ch. xxi. ver. 4, 'If his masters, (meaning his master) have given him a wife.' Verse 6, 'Then his masters, (that is, his master) shall bring him unto the Judges.' Ver. 29th, 'But if the ox were wont to push with his horn in time past, and it has been testified to his owners,' (that is, to his owner.) Isa. ch. vi. ver. 8, 'Whom shall I send? and who will go for us?' (that is, for me.)

"So also in the Qoran, 'We are (meaning I am) nearer than the jugular vein.' 'Surely *we* (meaning language was applied to the golden calf, which the children of Israel worshipped in the wilderness,—although it is very evident that there was but *one calf* made on that occasion. It is said, that the people brought their golden earrings to Aaron, "and he received them at their hand, and fashioned it with a graving tool, after he had made *it a molten calf:* and they said, *These be thy gods*, O Israel, which brought thee up out of the land of Egypt." Exodus xxxii. 4. The same plural language is repeated again in verse 8th, "These be thy gods, O Israel," etc. Aaron excused himself to Moses by saying, "They said unto me, make us *gods* which shall go before us."—verse 23. "And I said unto them, Whosoever hath any gold let them break it off. So they gave it me: then I cast it into the fire, and there came out *this calf.*"—verse 24. Can any rational mind pretend that the use of a plural noun and pronoun in this instance

---

I) created every thing in proportion.' In these two texts of the Qoran, God is represented to have spoken in the plural number, although Mohummud cannot be supposed to have employed a mode of expression which he could have supposed capable of being considered favourable to the Trinity.'

Appeal, etc., p. 140–143.

by the Israelites, proves that "*this calf*" was, in some sense, three calves, and at the same time only one calf?

The belief in one self-existent, eternal, omnipotent, and omnipresent God, was the great and fundamental doctrine of the Jewish religion; and the writings of the Old Testament are full of passages declaring that there is but one God, who is himself the Saviour and Redeemer of men. "I am the Lord," says he, "and there is none else—there is no God besides me."—"Thus saith the Lord, the Holy One of Israel, and his Maker." Is. xlv. 5, 11. "I, even I, am the Lord, and besides me there is no Saviour." "Thus saith the Lord, your Redeemer, the Holy One of Israel." Is. xliii. 11, 14. These sentiments are reiterated and confirmed in the New Testament. " Jesus answered, The first of all the commandments is, Hear, O Israel, the Lord our *God is one Lord.*" "And the scribes said unto him, Well, master, thou hast said the truth, for there is one God, and there is none other but he:" Mark xii. 29, 32; which proves that the Jews believed then, *as they do now*, that he is one undivided Deity.

We are told by the highest authority, that "none is good save one: that is God." Luke

xvii. 19. The apostle Paul says, "God is one." Gal. iii. 20. And the apostle Jude says, "To the only *wise God our Saviour*, be glory and majesty, dominion and power, both now and ever."—verse 25.

2. There are many names given to the Divine Being, in the Old and New Testaments, which are either expressive of his attributes, or descriptive of the various ways in which he has manifested himself to the children of men, according to their several states and capacities. Thus he is called Jehovah, or self-existing; and he is called Jah, which means eternal. He is also called the King of Glory, the Lord of Hosts, and the Prince of Peace. To the wicked he appears as a consuming fire; but to the faithful he becomes the Lord our righteousness, the Rock of ages, and the Saviour and Redeemer of his people. Yet, notwithstanding this variety of names which are given to the Divine Being, in both the Old and New Testaments, it is said by the prophet Zechariah, in allusion to the gospel day, "In that day there shall be *one Lord, and his name one.*" Chap. xiv. 9. Which I understand to mean, that there shall be *only one Divine power* acknowledged, to whom all these various names are attributed. The *name of the*

Lord is often used in scripture, to indicate the power or the presence of the Lord. Thus it is said, "The name of the Lord is a strong tower." Prov. xviii. 10. "Thy name is as ointment poured forth." Cant. i. 3. "For that thy *name is near* thy works declare." Ps. lxxv. 1. "Behold, I send an angel before thee to keep thee in the way. Beware of him, and obey his voice,—provoke him not, for he will not pardon your transgressions, for *my name is in him.*" Ex. xxiii. 20, 21.

From these and many other passages, I think it is clear, that to be baptized into the *name* of the Father, and of the Son, and of the Holy Ghost, signifies to be brought under the purifying influence of that *one Divine power*, whose manifestations to the children of men are represented by these various names. I see no reason to conclude that the Father, Son, and Holy Spirit, are all distinct persons, because these names are all found in one sentence.

There are many other places in the scriptures where the Divine Being is mentioned under different names in one sentence. For instance, "Unto us a child is born, unto us a son is given: and the government shall be upon his shoulder, and his *name* shall be called Wonderful, Counsellor, the Mighty God, the Everlasting Father, the Prince of Peace." Is. ix. 6. Here are five names mentioned, and, according to the trinitarian arguments, they imply *five persons* in the Deity. The reduplicative style is very common in the sacred writings. For example, the apostle James says: "Pure religion and undefiled before *God and the Father*, is this." — i. 27. And the apostle Paul says: "Do all in the *name* of the Lord Jesus, giving thanks to *God and the Father* by him." Colos. iii. 17. He also speaks in another place, "of *God, and of the Father, and of Christ.*" Col. ii. 2. From these expressions, some persons might conclude that *God and the Father* are two distinct persons; but the apostolic doctrine was, "There is but one God, the Father, *of* whom are all things, and we in him, and one Lord Jesus Christ, *by* whom are all things, and we by him." 1 Cor. viii. 6.

3. The attempt to prove that there are three persons in the Deity, by saying that different offices are assigned to the Father, and the Word, and the Holy Spirit, will not stand the test of scrutiny: for the scriptures ascribe precisely the same works to the Deity under each of these titles. For instance, the work of creation is

ascribed,—first, *to God:* "In the beginning God created the heaven and the earth." Gen. i. 1. Secondly, to the *Spirit of God:* "The Spirit of God moved upon the face of the waters." Gen. i. 2. "Thou sendest forth *thy spirit*, they are created; and thou renewest the face of the earth." Ps. civ. 30. Thirdly, to the *wisdom* of God: "By *wisdom* he made the heavens." Ps. cxxxvi. 5. "The Lord by *wisdom* hath founded the earth." Proverbs iii. 19. Fourthly, to the *Word of God:* "All things were made by him." John i. 3. "By the word of God the heavens were of old, and the earth standing out of the water and in the water." 2 Pet. iii. 5. Fifthly, to the *Son* of God: "He hath in these last days spoken unto us by his Son, by whom also he made the worlds." Heb. i. 2. "God created all things by Jesus Christ." Eph. iii. 9.

Here then, according to the trinitarian method of reasoning, are five persons concerned in the work of creation. But according to my view there is only one God, whose holy power or Divine influence is sometimes called the Spirit of God, or the Holy Spirit, because "God is a Spirit." It is sometimes called the Wisdom of God; for "in him are hid all the treasures of wisdom and knowledge." Col. ii. 3. It is likewise called the Word of God; because it is the medium by which he speaks to man. And it is called the Son of God, and Jesus Christ; because it was through this one Divine power that Jesus did the works of God. He said, "I can of mine own self do nothing; as I hear I judge, and my judgment is just, because I seek not mine own will, but the will of the Father which sent me." John v. 30. "The words that I speak unto you, I speak not of myself, but the Father that *dwelleth in me, he doeth the works.*" John xiv. 10.

4. This brings us to the last point of the argument, which relates to the union of the Divine and human natures in Jesus Christ. This union I fully acknowledge; but I can see no need of calling it a hypostatical union; for there is no such language used by the inspired writers, and I believe that this, and other Latin names, (such as trinity and triune God,) have been used as blinds, to conceal from the public the deplorable ignorance of priests and professors in relation to divine things. They being ignorant of "that wisdom which is from above," (James iii. 17,) have resorted to "the *words*

which man's wisdom teacheth," in order to appear wise before men.

The scriptures tell us, that "as many as are led by the Spirit of God, they are the sons of God." Romans viii. 14. "The Spirit itself beareth witness with our spirits, that we are the children of God: and if children, then heirs, heirs of God, and joint heirs with Christ."—verses 16, 17. They also teach us that we may become "partakers of the Divine nature." 2 Peter i. 4.

This union which takes place between God and all those who are born of his Spirit, is so perfect, that the church (or assembly of the righteous) is likened to a spiritual house, of which Christ is the "chief corner stone." 1 Peter ii. 5, 6. The apostle Paul, in addressing the Ephesians, says: "Ye are built upon the foundation of the apostles and prophets, Jesus Christ himself being the chief corner stone; in whom all the building, fitly framed together, groweth unto an holy temple in the Lord; in whom ye also are builded together, for an habitation of God through the Spirit." — ii. 20–22.

The church is also compared to a body, having many members, of which Jesus Christ is the *head*. (Eph. iv. 15.—Col. i. 18.—Romans xii. 4, 5.—1 Cor. xii. 12.) It appears to me, that the apostles considered "the man Christ Jesus," (1 Tim. ii. 5,) to be the chief member or head of the spiritual body, which is made up of the faithful servants of God of all ages and nations; and therefore they speak of him as the "first-born among many brethren." Rom. viii. 29.

With these views, I can fully acknowledge not only the Divine Word or Logos, which dwelt in Jesus without measure, and which constituted him the anointed Saviour, but I can likewise acknowledge the sinless perfection of his human nature. It appears from the scriptures that he was miraculously conceived and born of a virgin: he "was in all points tempted like as we are, yet without sin;" (Heb. iv. 15) and he was "a man approved of God, by miracles, and wonders, and signs, which God did by him." Acts ii. 22. It is, however, very evident, that the "two natures were distinct" in him; for it is not possible that the Divine nature should suffer death, or be affected with agony of soul.

I can further say with the apostle Paul, "Henceforth know we no man after the flesh; yea, though we have known Christ after the flesh, yet now henceforth know we him no more." 2 Cor. v. 16. And therefore, when I speak of Christ Jesus, or the Saviour, I mean that "unction from the *Holy One*," which reigned in Jesus, and "the manifestation" of which "is given to every man to profit withal:" (1 Cor. xii. 7) for, "of his fulness have all we received, and grace for grace." John i. 16. "In him was life, and the life was the light of men.— That was the true light which lighteth every man that cometh into the world."—ver. 4. 9.*

This Divine power, or word of God, is often called Christ by the writers of the New Testament. For instance, Paul says of the children of Israel under Moses, that "they did all eat the same spiritual meat, and they did all drink the same spiritual drink; for they drank of that spiritual rock that followed them, and *that rock was Christ.*" 1 Cor. x. 4.

Peter says that the prophets "prophesied of

---

* "I said that we believed in Christ, both as he was the man Jesus, and God over all, blessed forever.— And I am sure that Paul divides him more than we did, (Romans ix. 5,) since he makes a distinction between Christ as God and Christ as man." Wm. Penn's Letter to George Fox. See Janney's Life of Penn, 2d edition, p. 101.

the grace that should come unto you, searching what, or what manner of time, the spirit of Christ which was in them did signify; when it testified beforehand of the sufferings of Christ, and the glory that should follow." 1 Pet. i. 11. There are a great many other passages in the New Testament, where Christ is spoken of as that one Divine Spirit who manifests himself *in man* for our sanctification and redemption. For example: "Know ye not your own selves, how that Jesus Christ is in you, except ye be reprobates." 2 Cor. xiii. 5. "To whom God would make known what is the riches of the glory of this mystery among the Gentiles, which is Christ in you the hope of glory." Col. i. 27. "It pleased God to reveal his Son in me, that I might preach him among the heathen." Gal. i. 15, 16. "Ye are not in the flesh but in the spirit, if so be that the *Spirit of God* dwell in you. Now if any man have not the *Spirit of Christ* he is none of his." Rom. viii. 9. Here the Spirit of God and the Spirit of Christ are spoken of as one and the same.

In confirmation of this, the apostle goes on to say, "And if Christ be in you, the body is dead because of [or as to] sin; but the spirit is alive, because of righteousness. But if the

Spirit of him that raised up Jesus Christ from the dead, dwell in you, he that raised up Christ from the dead, shall also quicken your mortal bodies by his Spirit that dwelleth in you."—ver. 10, 11. The same apostle says, "Because ye are sons, God hath sent forth the spirit of his Son into your hearts, crying Abba, Father."— Gal. iv. 6. And again he says, "The Lord is that Spirit, and where the Spirit of the Lord is, there is liberty." 2 Cor. iii. 17. I might adduce many other passages, to show that when the apostles speak of Christ, they often mean the *anointing power* of God's Spirit, or "the law of the spirit of life in Christ Jesus, which makes free from the law of sin and death," that " wars in our members." Rom. viii. 2, and viii. 23. It is evident, that Jesus spake of his outward body merely as a temple in which this Divine power was manifested; for he said, " Destroy this temple, and in three days *I will* raise it up." " But he spake of the temple of his body." John ii. 19–21. In this prediction he spoke in the name of his Father; for it is said in the scriptures that " he was raised up from the dead by the *glory of the Father.*"— Rom. vi. 4. " This commandment have I received of my Father." John x. 18. And after he was risen, he said to Mary, "Go to my brethren, and say unto them, I ascend unto my Father and your Father, and to my God and your God." John xx. 17.

John. It appears that the same body which was crucified, rose again and ascended up to heaven, and now sitteth on the right hand of God; for he said, after his resurrection, "A spirit hath not flesh and bones, as ye see me have:" which shows that it was a human body. And it is also said, "He was taken up, and a cloud received him out of their sight."— Acts i. 9.

James. I think the circumstance of his being received up into *a cloud*, does not prove that the same body of *flesh and bones* was introduced into the spiritual world. As God is a pure "Spirit, without body, parts, or passions,"* it is very possible that he changed his Son into his own likeness, or that he gave him a spiritual body. When Elijah was translated, he was taken up by a chariot of fire and horses of fire, but I do not conclude from this, that there are horses in heaven. I consider it a striking evidence of

---

* Episcopal Articles.

Divine power displayed on this occasion, to confirm the faith of Elisha.

Jesus taught the Jews that Abraham, Isaac, and Jacob, were *then* living. Matthew xxii. 32. Yet we have no reason to believe that their *earthly bodies* ever had been raised from the grave. What I understand by the resurrection, as regards a future existence, is the soul being raised out of this state of mutability into a spiritual world, where it shall receive either happiness or misery, " according to the deeds done in the body."

Father. Perhaps we had best not indulge in much speculation on this subject, for " secret things belong unto the Lord our God, but the things which are revealed belong unto us and our children."

The apostle Paul, on the subject of the resurrection, says: " Now this I say, brethren, that flesh and blood cannot inherit the kingdom of God." 1 Cor. xv. 50. And the apostle John writes with still more caution, for he says, " Beloved, now are we the sons of God, and it doth not *yet appear* what we shall be; but when he cometh we shall be like him, for we shall see him as he is; and every man that hath this hope in him, purifieth himself, even as he is pure."

1 John iii. 2, 3. This ought to be the main object of our thoughts, to purify ourselves even as he is pure, in order that we may become the sons of God. "My little children," saith the apostle, "of whom I travail in birth again until Christ be formed in you." Gal. iv. 19. "There is one body, and one spirit, even as you are called in one hope of your calling; one Lord, one faith, one baptism, one God and Father of all, who is above all, through all, and in you all. But unto every one of us is given grace according to the measure of the gift of Christ." Eph. iv. 4–7. "Till we all come, in the unity of the faith and of the knowledge of the Son of God, unto a perfect man, unto the measure of the stature of the fulness of Christ." — verse 13. This stature of the fulness of Christ consists, I believe, in a state of perfect obedience to the law of Divine love, by which means our minds may become so transformed by the spirit of Christ, as to be in unity with him, even as he is in unity with the Father; agreeably to the prayer of the blessed Jesus, when he said, "Holy Father, keep through thine *own name*, those whom thou hast given me that they may be *one* as we are. As thou, Father, art in me, and I in thee, that they may be one in us."—

John xvii. 11, 21. "I will pray the Father," said he, "and he shall give you another Comforter, that he may abide with you for ever, even the Spirit of truth, whom the world cannot receive because it seeth him not, neither knoweth him: but ye know him, for he dwelleth *with* you, and shall be *in* you. I will not leave you comfortless, I will come to you." John xiv. 16–18.

Here we see that the same Holy Spirit which was in Jesus, and thus dwelt *with* the disciples, was to be manifested *in them*, for their comfort; and not unto them only, but unto as many as should believe on him through their word.

John. If we consider the Divine Word, or Spirit of Christ, to be the medium through which God reveals himself to man, does not this seem to imply that there are two Divine powers or persons?

Father. I will answer this question by asking another. What do men generally understand by the term nature, when they speak of the laws of nature and the powers of nature?— Do they mean that there is another power besides that of God operating upon the material world?

John. I understand by it nothing more than

the power of God, as continually displayed in the outward creation.

Father. And so, when I speak of Christ, or the Divine Word, I mean "the power of God and the wisdom of God," (1 Cor. i 24,) *as manifested in the souls of men*, to redeem them from all iniquity, and to bring them into his own glorious image of purity and love. This Divine power is represented under various figures or metaphors, in the scriptures; but the most striking and beautiful, is that of light. The apostle John says, "God is light, and in him is no darkness at all." And speaking of Christ, he says, "In him was life, and the life was the light of men; that was the true light, which ligheth every man that cometh into the world." God is the great luminary or sun of his spiritual creation; and that power or influence by which he acts upon the souls of men, is called his light : " For whatsoever *doth make manifest is light.* Wherefore he saith, Awake thou that sleepest, and arise from the dead, and *Christ shall give thee light.*" Eph. v. 13, 14. As the light of the sun is the source of all the beauty that adorns the outward creation, and as the smallest ray of light contains in itself every colour of the rainbow; so this Divine light which emanates from God, is the source of every Christian virtue, and "in it are hidden all the treasures of wisdom and knowledge."

When we see such striking evidences of Divine power and goodness displayed in the government of the outward world, — clothing the earth with flowers and verdure in spring, with harvests in summer, and with fruits in autumn,— and preserving the various tribes of animals through the severity of winter: when we feel assured that not even a sparrow falls to the ground without his notice;—can we suppose that he withdraws his presence from the immortal part of his creature man? No; it is on the rational soul of man that he bestows his peculiar care; it is there that his sensible presence is felt, and to him alone are we indebted for every holy aspiration after virtue, and every feeling of extended benevolence. And he not only incites us to goodness, but he reproves us for evil, and, as a tender father, he visits and revisits his erring children with "the reproofs of instruction, which are the way of life."

" Thou art the source and centre of all minds,
    Their only point of rest, *Eternal Word!*
    From thee departing they are lost, and rove
    At random, without honour, hope, or peace.

From thee is all that soothes the life of man;
His high endeavour, and his glad success,
His strength to suffer, and his will to serve.
But O thou bounteous Giver of all good,
Thou art of all thy gifts thyself the crown!
Give what thou canst, without thee we are poor;
And with thee rich, take what thou wilt away."

COWPER.

NOTE.

There is one text which was not introduced nor alluded to in the foregoing conversation, because its authenticity is now considered so doubtful that it has been abandoned by some of the most learned biblical critics. The following remarks in relation to it are extracted from the commentary of Adam Clarke, a learned trinitarian writer.

1 John v. 7. "For there are three that bear record in heaven, the Father, the Word, and the Holy Ghost; and these three are one."

"There are one hundred and thirteen Greek MSS. extant, containing the first epistle of John, and this text is *wanting in one hundred and twelve.* It only exists in the Codex Montfortii, (a comparatively recent MS.,) already described."

"All the Greek fathers omit the verse, though

many of them quote both verse 6th and 8th, applying them to the Trinity, Divinity of Christ, and the Holy Spirit."

"The first place the verse appears in Greek, is in the Greek translation of the acts of the council of Lateran, held A. D. 1215."

"The Latin fathers do not quote it, even where it would have greatly strengthened their arguments, and where, had it existed, it might have been most naturally expected. It is wanting in all the ancient versions, the Vulgate excepted; but the most ancient copies of this have it not."

"It is wanting in the German translation of Luther, and in all the editions of it published during his lifetime. It is inserted in our *early* English translations, but with marks of doubtfulness."

"In short, it stands on no authority, sufficient to authenticate any part of a revelation professing to have come from God."

See, also, Griesbach's Greek Testament.

CONVERSATION V.

ON SALVATION BY CHRIST.

James. In our last conversation, the attributes of the Divine Being and the Divinity of Christ, were discussed; and now I feel desirous of being better informed respecting the Christian doctrine of salvation.

Father. This is the most important subject that can possibly engage our attention; and we ought each one of us to take it into serious consideration, and endeavour to know by experience what it is to be saved from sin. It is an individual work; for "no man can save his brother, nor give to God a ransom for his soul;" but we must all "work out our own salvation with fear and trembling." Phil. ii. 12.

John. I should think this last quotation is not to be taken so literally as to imply that we can work out our own salvation without Divine assistance.

Father. Certainly not. It only means that we should accept the offers of Divine grace, and heartily co-operate therewith: for the apostle says in the next verse, "It is God which worketh in you, both to will and to do of his good pleasure." After all that we can do, our salvation must be attributed to God: for although it cannot be done without us, it is equally certain that it cannot be done of ourselves. "By grace are ye saved, through faith, and that not of yourselves; it is the gift of God." Eph. ii. 8.

The first point to be considered in this inquiry is, What is salvation? I think all must acknowledge, that it is a deliverance from the *guilt* and *dominion* of sin; and consequently an exemption from the misery that is entailed upon sin, both here and hereafter. This view is confirmed by the whole tenor of the sacred writings; and it appears that the special object of Christ's mission was "to save his people *from their sins.*" Matt. i. 21. A man cannot be truly said to be *saved from his sins*, while he is living in the daily practice of sinning. For "he that doeth righteousness is righteous;" but "he that committeth sin is of the devil." 1 John iii. 7, 8. The next inquiry is, What is sin? The apostle John answers, "Sin is the transgression of the law." 1 John iii. 4. Well, what law is it that we are now living under? It is not the law of Moses; but the law of the new covenant, which is *written in the heart.*—For, "this is the covenant that I will make with the house of Israel after those days, saith the Lord; I will put my *laws into their mind*, and *write them in their hearts;* and I will be to them a God and they shall be to me a people; and they shall not teach every man his neighbour, and every man his brother, saying, Know the Lord: for all shall know me, from the least to the greatest. For I will be merciful to their unrighteousness, and their sins and their iniquities will I remember no more." Heb. viii. 10. Jer. xxxi. 33. It appears then, that sin is the transgression of this holy law: "for if our heart condemn us, God is greater than our heart, and knoweth all things;" but "if our heart condemn us not, then have we confidence towards God." 1 John iii. 20, 21.

Now if we will revert to our own experience, we shall find that every transgression of this law written in the heart, is followed by condemnation and disquietude: for the Divine Author of our being has so constituted the human mind, that we never can be happy while in a state of disobedience to his holy law; therefore he says, "Thine own wickedness shall correct thee, and thy backslidings shall reprove thee." Jer. ii. 19. "Say ye to the righteous, it shall be well with him; for they shall eat the fruit of their doings: but wo unto the wicked, it shall be ill with him; for the reward of his hands shall be given him." Isa. iii. 10. "The work of righteousness shall be peace, and the effect of righteousness, quietness, and assurance for ever." Isa. xxxii. 17. This "peace of God, which passeth understanding;" this holy joy and serenity of mind, which springs from "the *love of God shed abroad in the heart,*" is the only thing that can fill and satisfy the cravings of an immortal soul, which pants for the joys of eternal life. How important then is the inquiry, What is it that separates us from the Divine harmony, and cuts us off from the joys of paradise? "Behold," says the prophet, "your *iniquities* have separated between you and your God, and your sins have hid his face from you." Isa. liv. 1. If sin separates the soul from God, it is clear that we cannot be united to him while we continue to be sinful: for "what communion is there between light and darkness? — what concord between Christ and Belial?" But "thanks be to God for his unspeakable gift!" He not only sent his beloved Son into the world to "save his people *from* their sins," and to "destroy the works of the devil," (1 John iii. 8,) but he still reveals himself to man as a God " nigh at hand, a very present help in time of trouble;" and it is "through his mercy that he *saves us, by the washing* of regeneration and renewing of the Holy Ghost." All he requires of man is, to repent of his sins by *turning away from them,* and to become obedient to " the law of the spirit of life in Christ Jesus, which makes free from the law of sin and death." This "law of sin and death," is the law which "wars in our members," (Rom. vii. 23, viii. 2,) and consists of "the lusts of the flesh, the lusts of the eyes, and the pride of life, which are not of the Father, but of the world." It is needful that the power of God should be revealed *in man*, to overcome these spiritual enemies; and therefore his holy Word, or Spirit of truth, is sent to "convince the world of sin, of righteousness, and of judgment." This is that "grace of *God which bringeth salvation,* and hath *appeared unto all men,* teaching us, that denying ungodliness and worldly lusts, we should live soberly, righteously, and godly in this present world."

He who lives in obedience to this Spirit of truth, or grace of God, will find a continual growth and increase of strength, by which he will be enabled to resist temptation and to work righteousness; until, at length, it will become his study and delight to do the Father's will, and glorify his name on earth. This is the Emmanuel state, in which God becomes the life of the soul: for he is the Alpha and the Omega, the beginning and the end of our salvation. "I am the Lord," he says, "and besides me there is no Saviour." Isa. xliii. 3, 11. "I am a just God and a Saviour: there is none besides me." Isa. xlv. 15, 21, xlix. 26, lx. 16. Hos. xiii. 4. Therefore, unto him, "the only wise God our Saviour, be glory and majesty, dominion and power, both now and for ever."—Jude 25.

John. These views appear to be consistent with the scriptures, as far as they go; but it seems to me that a very important doctrine of Christianity still remains to be considered. I mean the doctrine of atonement.

Father. I have been speaking of what I consider the doctrine of atonement or reconciliation. For it is admitted even by trinitarian writers, that "the doctrine of atonement, as far as relates to sin, is nothing more than the doctrine of reconciliation." And indeed, in a sense agreeable to this, that of bringing into a state of concord and reconciliation, the word atonement itself had been originally used by our old English writers, with whom, according to Junius Skinner, and Johnson, it was written *at-one-ment;* — signifying to be *at-one,* or to come to an agreement. [*See Magee on Atonement*, pp. 184, 186.]

Now, it appears to me that God is altogether unchangeable himself, and perfectly pure and holy; and therefore, the sinner cannot be in a state of *concord and reconciliation* with him, until his sinful nature is removed by "the washing of regeneration and renewing of the Holy Ghost." Thus, " putting off the old man with his deeds, and putting on the new man, which is renewed in knowledge, *after the image* of him that created him." Col. iii. 9, 10.

John. What I mean by the doctrine of atonement, is a belief in the *vicarious sufferings* of Jesus Christ, when he suffered death without the gates of Jerusalem, as a *substitute* for the whole human race; in order to satisfy the offended justice of God, and to render him propitious to guilty man. Adam, and all his posterity, having broken the law of God, it would have been necessary for the whole human race to have suffered eternal death, in order to satisfy the infinite justice of God; but the Son of God offered himself as a substitute for man, and agreed to pay the price of our redemption, by taking on him a human body, and suffering the pains of death.

Father. As I said on a former occasion, those who profess to derive their doctrines entirely from the scriptures, ought to be very careful to adhere strictly to the text. Now we find no such language in the scriptures, as the *vicarious* sufferings of Jesus Christ; nor do they say that he died as a *substitute* for guilty man; nor is there any language in them, from which such a conclusion can be fairly drawn. To punish the innocent, in order that the guilty may go free, is entirely inconsistent with the justice and mercy of the Divine character. "He that justifieth the wicked, and he that condemneth the just, even they both are abomination to the Lord." Prov. xvii. 15. It is said in the scriptures, that Christ died for all men; but there is not the slightest intimation that his sufferings were intended to appease the wrath, or satisfy the justice of God. The object of his mission was to bear witness to the truth. "To this end was I born," said he, "and for this cause came I into the world, that I should bear witness unto the truth." John xviii. 37. But he could not bear witness to the truth, among that perverse and wicked generation, without exposing himself to sufferings and death; and he therefore laid down his life for the salvation of mankind.— His death did not change the feelings nor the purposes of God towards mankind; for God is altogether unchangeable. In him is neither variableness nor shadow of turning:" and he is always "kind, even to the unthankful and to the evil."

The mission of Jesus Christ was itself the effect of God's unchanging love to man; for all the good that he did, was done by the power of God operating through him. "I can of myself do nothing," said he; "my Father that dwelleth in me he doeth the works." "God was in Christ, reconciling the world unto himself, not imputing their trespasses unto them, and hath committed unto us the word of reconciliation. Now then, we are ambassadors for Christ," says the apostle, "as though God did beseech you by us; we pray you in Christ's stead, be ye *reconciled* to God." 2 Cor. v. 19, 20. There is not a word said in the scriptures, about God being *reconciled* to man by the death of his Son; but it is man that must be reconciled to God; for he has always loved mankind: but man being at enmity with him, it is in *man* that the change *must* be wrought, and the reconciliation effected. One means which the Divine Being has made use of, in all ages of the world, to change the hearts of wicked men, has been the patience, the resignation, and the joy with which his faithful servants have suffered for his cause, when persecuted by the wicked. It was in this way that Jesus Christ and his apostles bore their testimony to the truth, and exemplified before men the goodness, the purity, and the love of that Divine Power, whose kingdom was established within them. It was in this way, too, that the primitive Christians, though generally poor, illiterate, and despised among men, were made the instruments of convincing mankind, and enlarging the Redeemer's kingdom. And if the kingdoms of this world shall ever "become the kingdoms of God and of his Christ," (as I believe they will,) it must be effected by the holy living, the meek example, and the patient sufferings of the faithful. I can conceive of no other means so well calculated to touch the feelings and to convince the judgment, as the example of one who is actuated by the love of God in all things, and who is willing to "lay down his life for the brethren," and for the testimony of truth.

We find that the holy living, the powerful preaching, and the numerous miracles of Jesus, made but few converts, until he "laid down his life for the sheep," and sealed his testimony with his blood. It was then that many began to perceive that "his kingdom was not of this world, else would his servants fight." They were convinced that he had been actuated by Divine love in all that he did: and when the apostles, who were filled with the Holy Spirit, began to preach to the multitude, and showed them that "God had made that same Jesus whom they had crucified, both Lord and Christ," then "they were pricked in their hearts, and said unto Peter and to the rest of the apostles, Men and brethren, what shall we do?" Acts ii. 36, 37. And "the same day there were added unto them about three thousand souls."—verse 41.

Thus we see how the sufferings of the Messiah operated upon the people of that day, to reconcile them to God; but it is the life and power of God that dwelt in Christ, which *saves* from sin: "for if when we were enemies," says the apostle Paul, "we were reconciled to God by the death of his Son, much more, being reconciled, we shall be *saved by his life.*" Rom. v. 10. For "in him was life, and the life was the light of men." John i. 4. It is this life of God, or "Spirit of truth" revealed in the soul, which purifies and saves from sin. This life is sometimes spoken of as the blood; for according to the Jewish law "the blood is the life." (Levit. xvii. 11, 14,—Gen. ix. 4,—Deut. xii. 23.) And when Jesus told the people, "Except ye eat the flesh of the Son of man, and drink his blood, ye have no life in you;" he did not allude to the flesh and blood of his outward body, but to the life and power of God which dwelt in him, and spake through him.— In confirmation of this view, he said himself to his disciples, by way of explanation, "It is the Spirit which quickeneth; the flesh profiteth nothing: the words that I speak unto you, they are spirit, and they are life." John vi. 53, 63.

When the apostle John saw, in the Revelations, "a great multitude which no man could number, of all nations, and kindreds, and people, and tongues, who stood before the throne and before the Lamb, clothed with white robes, and palms in their hands," he was told, that these were they who had "come out of great tribulation," who had "washed their robes and made them white in the blood of the Lamb." Rev. vii. 9, 14. Now, we cannot suppose that these robes were made of earthly materials; nor will any one contend that the blood with which they were washed and *made white,* was the outward blood shed upon mount Calvary. They were spiritual garments, and the blood too was spiritual; it was the life or spirit of God which dwelt in Jesus; and it is by this only that our hearts can be " sprinkled from an evil conscience."— For "if the blood of bulls and of goats, and the ashes of an heifer, sprinkling the unclean, sanctifieth to the purifying of the flesh; how much more shall the blood of Christ, who, through the eternal Spirit, offered himself without spot to God, purge your conscience from dead works to serve the living God!" Heb. ix. 13, 14. It appears very evident to me, that nothing of an outward character can purge the conscience, or purify the mind; for these are spiritual, and require spiritual agents to act upon them.

John. It appears to me that in this last quotation, the apostle alludes to the Jewish sacrifices of bulls and goats, as being the types of that great sacrifice which Christ was to make of himself once for all. The sacrifice of the scape-goat, once in the year, on the day of solemn expiation for the sins of the whole people, is generally considered a striking type of the sacrifice of Christ, which it was intended to prefigure. Two goats were brought to the door of the tabernacle for a sin-offering, and the high priest cast lots upon them, which should be sacrificed to the Lord and which should be set at liberty. One of them was then put to death for a sin-offering for all the people, his blood was sprinkled upon the altar, and his body was burnt without the camp. The other was the scape-goat, on which the high-priest laid his hands, confessing his sins and the sins of all the people; he then sent him into the wilderness, to a place not inhabited, to be there set at liberty, and to bear the iniquities of the people.— The first of these goats is supposed to have been intended to prefigure the death of Christ; and the second, which was saved alive, to typify his resurrection.

Father. We are not informed in any part of the scriptures, that these goats were intended as types of Jesus Christ, and I can see no reason for such a conclusion. There are, however, several reasons which have convinced me that they had no such meaning. In the first place, the goat was never made use of as an emblem of purity or holiness; but, on the contrary, always as an emblem of sin; for our Saviour himself spoke of it in this way, when he said he would place the sheep on his right hand, and the goats (that is, the wicked) on his left. 2. The Messiah is spoken of under the figure of a lamb; and it is not possible that he could be typified by two natures so entirely opposite as the lamb and the goat. 3. It appears to me that these sacrifices were figures of spiritual things, and that the holy men of old understood them in that light; for we find that the more enlightened they became, the less reliance they placed upon these outward ceremonies.

The prophet Samuel said to Saul, "Hath the Lord as great delight in burnt offerings and sacrifices, as in obeying the voice of the Lord? Behold, to obey is better than sacrifice, and to hearken than the fat of rams." 1 Samuel xv. 22. The prophet Isaiah told the people that the Lord had no pleasure in their sacrifices, because their "hands were full of blood," and he exhorts them, in the name of the Most High, to put away the evil of their doings.—"Cease to do evil, learn to do well; seek judgment, relieve the oppressed; judge the fatherless, plead for the widow. Come now, and let us reason together, saith the Lord; though your sins be as scarlet, they shall be as white as snow; though they be red like crimson, they shall be as wool." But the language of Jeremiah is still more decided against placing any dependence upon outward sacrifices. "Thus saith the Lord of hosts, the God of Israel: Put your burnt offerings unto your sacrifices, and eat flesh. For I spake not unto your fathers, nor commanded them in the day that I brought them out of the land of Egypt, concerning burnt-offerings or sacrifices: but this thing commanded I them, saying, Obey my voice, and I will be your God, and ye shall be my people; and walk in all the ways that I have commanded you, that it may be well with you."— Jer. vii. 21–23.

King David, when he had committed a great sin, exclaimed in the depth of his contrition, "Create in me a clean heart, O God, and renew a right spirit within me. Cast me not away from thy presence, and take not thy holy Spirit from me. Restore unto me the joy of thy sal-

vation, and uphold me with thy free spirit."—
" Thou desirest not *sacrifice*, else would I give it; thou delightest not in *burnt-offerings*. The sacrifices of God are a broken spirit; a *broken and a contrite heart*, O God, thou wilt not despise." Ps. li. 10–12, 16, 17.

It appears that whenever an animal was sacrificed according to the Mosaic law, the blood was sprinkled upon the altar; " for the life of the flesh is in the blood, and I have given it to you upon the altar, to make an atonement for the soul. Therefore, I said unto the children of Israel, No soul of you shall eat blood, neither shall any stranger that sojourneth among you eat blood." Lev. xvii. 11. Now, "it is not possible," says the apostle Paul, " that the blood of bulls and of goats should take away sins."— Heb. x. 4. Therefore, the hearts of the people were not purified by those offerings, unless they came to experience in themselves that "sacrifice of God, a broken and a contrite spirit," which these outward offerings were intended to represent. For as the blood of beasts, which is the life thereof, was to be sacrificed to God; so the carnal nature in man, or the life of the flesh, must be sacrificed by being broken and contrited before the Lord, through the power of his spirit. "They that are Christ's," says the apostle Paul, "have crucified the flesh with its affections and lusts." Gal. v. 24. "Our old man is crucified with him, that the body of sin might be destroyed, that henceforth we should not serve sin." Rom. vi. 6. This "old man," or carnal nature in man, is predominant in every individual when he has placed his affections upon earthly things, and become subject to the "lusts of the flesh, the lusts of the eye, and the pride of life, which are not of the Father, but of the world." If, then, we would be redeemed from these things, we must be willing to submit to the death of the cross; that is, to have all our animal appetites, and all our selfish desires, subjected to the power of God which is revealed within. For the cross of Christ is the power of God; and it is by this power that we must be "crucified to the world, and the world unto us." This "death unto sin," takes place in all who come to know Christ "the resurrection and the life." "I protest by your rejoicing," says the apostle, "which I have in Christ Jesus our Lord, I die daily." 1 Corinth. xv. 31. "I am crucified with Christ: nevertheless I live; yet not I, but Christ liveth in me." Gal. ii. 20. Know ye not that as many as are baptized into

Christ, are baptized into his death. Rom. vi. 3. This death is not the death of the outward body; for he says of Christ, "In that he died, he *died* unto sin once; but in that he liveth, he liveth unto God." Rom. vi. 10. How did he die unto sin? Was it not by suppressing or subduing the first motions or propensities to sin, as they rose in his heart? "For we have not an high priest that cannot be touched with the feeling of our infirmities; but was in all points tempted like as we are, yet without sin." Heb iv. 15. And how are we tempted? The apostle James tells us, "Let no man say when he is tempted, I am tempted of God; for God cannot be tempted with evil, neither tempteth he any man: but every man is tempted when he is drawn away of his own lusts, (or desires,) and enticed. Then when lust hath conceived it bringeth forth sin; and sin when finished, bringeth forth death." These desires and propensities of our nature do not become sinful until they are perverted from their original purpose; and in Jesus Christ they never did become so, for he kept them all in subjection to the will of God. They are all good when kept under the Divine government; for they are then calculated to subserve those purposes for which they were created. Like the animals in paradise, they are all at peace with man, and in obedience to him. And the reign of Christ is intended to bring us back to that state in which "the wolf shall dwell with the lamb, and the leopard shall lie down with the kid, and the calf, and the young lion, and the fatling together, and a little child shall lead them." Isa. xi. 6. While man remained in paradise, in a state of innocence, he offered no animals in sacrifice to God; for these were only added or introduced because of transgression: and when Jesus Christ appeared to promulgate and exemplify the new-covenant dispensation, he took away the hand-writing of ordinances, and showed that the whole intention of the old law was fulfilled in loving God supremely, and our neighbour as ourselves: for "on these two commandments hang all the law and the prophets." Matthew xxii. 40.

The old covenant, being an outward law, the vessels used in the service of the temple, and the priests with their garments, were purified by sprinkling with outward blood, "which is the life of the flesh;" but the new covenant, being an inward law, "placed in the mind, and written in the heart," (Heb. viii. 10,) it was necessary that the soul itself should be purified with better offerings than these,—even with "the blood of the Lamb," which is the life or spirit of Christ revealed in us.

James. As the mind of man is spiritual, it appears very plain to me, that it cannot be washed or purified by any thing of an external nature. If "nothing that goeth into the mouth *defileth* the man," it is equally plain that nothing that is taken into the mouth, or applied to the body, can *purify* the man from sin. And it is equally impossible that any outward sacrifice could produce a change in the Divine mind; for we have abundant evidence that he is "the same yesterday, to-day, and forever," and that he is always waiting to be gracious to the repenting sinner. His dealings with man are beautifully exemplified in the parable of the prodigal son, who had wandered far from his father's house, and spent his substance in riotous living. When he came to himself, and determined to go back to his father, confessing his sins and offering to become as one of the hired servants, his father did not stand off and order him to be punished, neither did he lay his punishment upon the other son who had been faithful; but his compassion was awakened by his penitence and the sufferings he had already brought upon himself, and "while he was yet a great way off, he ran and fell on his neck and kissed him." Luke xv. 20.

Father. The character of the parent, as represented in this parable, answers exactly to my view of the Divine character, and it corresponds entirely with the character of Jesus Christ, who was filled with the Divine perfections. But the doctrine that God cannot, or will not forgive sins without a compensation, and that man not being able to make this compensation, it was made by Jesus Christ, who was appointed or given up to be *killed for this purpose,* is so inconsistent with the Divine character, that I cannot reconcile it to my feelings; — it appears to me to deprive the Deity of that infinite love which is his most endearing attribute: and if a human parent were to act upon the same principles towards his children, we could not justify his conduct.

John. The advocates of this doctrine say, it was necessary that the *infinite* justice of God should be satisfied for the sin of Adam, and for our sins; and they allege, that man being *finite,* could not make an *infinite* satisfaction.

Father. But I cannot see how man, who is finite, could commit an infinite offence; and if nothing less than infinite satisfaction would answer, then God must die to *satisfy his own justice;* for he is the only infinite Being. But this conclusion is too absurd to be for a moment admitted.*

John. It was only the human nature which was united to God, that died. It is impossible for the Deity to die.

Father. If, then, it was only human nature that died, what becomes of the *infinite satisfaction?* It is clear to my mind, that when the *sinful nature in man is slain* by the power or word of God being raised into dominion *in us,*

---

* On this subject, Wm. Penn writes as follows:— " I can boldly challenge any person to give me one scripture phrase which does approach the doctrine of *satisfaction,* (much less the name), considering to what degree it is stretched: not that we do deny, but really confess, that Jesus Christ, in life, doctrine, and death, fulfilled his Father's will and offered up a most satisfactory sacrifice; but not to pay God or help him (as otherwise being unable) to save man; and for a justification by an *imputative righteousness,* whilst not real, it is really an imagination, not a reality, and therefore rejected; otherwise confessed and known to be justifying before God, because there is no abiding in Christ's love without keeping his commandments."— *Sandy Foundation Shaken, conclusion.*

then is the Divine justice satisfied; for there is nothing vindictive in the character of the Deity. He does not afflict his creatures for any other purpose than their own reformation; and when that reformation is effected, he is always ready to pardon his repenting children. Even among men, the reformation of criminals is now considered by the humane to be the main object of all the punishments inflicted upon them; and if we could be certain, in any case, that a thorough change of heart had been effected, it would be our duty to receive back the offender into society. But God can see the heart; and he not only sees it, but his spirit still strives with man, in order to reclaim him from the evil of his ways; and we have the assurance that he takes no pleasure in the death of a sinner, but desires that he may return, repent, and live.— "If the wicked will turn from all the sins that he hath committed, and keep all my statutes, and do that which is lawful and right, he shall surely live, he shall not die; all his transgressions that he hath committed, they shall not be mentioned unto him." Ezek. xviii. 21. "If we confess our sins, he is faithful and just to forgive us our sins, and to cleanse us from all unrighteousness." 1 John i. 9.

This is a very different view of Divine justice from that which too generally prevails in Christendom. The doctrines of imputative sin, and imputative righteousness, appear to me to be derogatory to the Divine character; and I think they must have an injurious effect upon the human mind, because they have a tendency to blind or obliterate all the distinctions of right and wrong. In the first place, this *scheme*, as it is called, charges upon the whole human race, even upon little children, the guilt of Adam's transgression. In the second place, it transfers all his guilt, by imputation, to Jesus Christ, the pure and spotless Son of God; and what is still more absurd, it imputes the righteousness of Christ to all mankind who can believe that he died as their substitute. Now, I believe that God regards every human soul without respect of persons. He sees the wicked as they are, and likewise the righteous; and his language still is, "The righteousness of the righteous shall be upon him, and the wickedness of the wicked shall be upon him." Exek. xviii. 20. The only true ground of acceptance, is the newbirth: for when Christ's kingdom is established within us, then his righteousness becomes ours; not by imputation, but by our becoming really "partakers of the Divine nature."

John. There are several passages in the scriptures which appear to militate against these views, and to confirm those which I advanced; and I cannot see how they can be explained in any other way. I think Christ is often spoken of as a sacrifice offered to God; it is said, "he was once offered to bear the sins of many." "He hath made him to be sin for us, who knew no sin, that we might be made the righteousness of God in him." "Christ also hath once suffered, the just for the unjust, that he might bring us to God." The prophet Isaiah says, "Surely he hath borne our griefs, and carried our sorrows; yet did we esteem him stricken, smitten of God, and afflicted. But he was wounded for our transgressions, he was bruised for our iniquities, the chastisement of our peace was upon him, and with his stripes we are healed. All we, like sheep, have gone astray, we have turned every one to his own way, and the Lord hath laid on him the iniquities of us all."—This language must allude to Christ, for the apostle Peter quotes it and applies it to him: "Who his own self bare our sins in his own body on the tree." 1 Peter ii. 24.

Father. It is true that the death of the Messiah is often spoken of as a sacrifice offered to God; but the same term is applied by the apostle Paul to his own expected martyrdom: for he says, "I am ready to be offered." 2 Tim. iv. 6. And again he says, "If I be offered upon the sacrifice and service of your faith, I joy and rejoice with you all." Phil. ii. 17. The same kind of figurative language is still used, but no one ever thinks of taking it literally. For instance, it may be said that many of the reformers *sacrificed their lives* in the cause of truth; and that religious liberty has been purchased with the blood of the martyrs. We all know how to understand this language, and why may we not conclude that the Jews used it in the same sense? It is very obvious that Paul used it in this sense, when he spoke of himself being offered up as a sacrifice.

The other passages which speak of the Messiah bearing the sins of many; being made sin for us; suffering for the unjust; and having laid on him the iniquity of all, — will admit of a very different interpretation from that which has been given to them by the advocates of a vicarious atonement, and one that is far more consistent with the Divine character. They do not say that the sins of others were imputed to him, nor that he suffered, as a substitute, the punishment that was due to others. I take it that he bore the sufferings which the iniquity of the Jews inflicted upon him; and these sufferings were both mental and corporeal. "He became a man of sorrows, and acquainted with grief." He was baptized into a state of deep sympathy and suffering for a fallen world. I have no doubt that the agony he endured in the garden, was owing to the deep sense he then had of the wickedness of man; for he said, "My soul is exceeding sorrowful, even unto death." These spiritual sufferings appear to have been experienced in some degree by the apostles, when they afterwards became "baptized into Christ," and were "buried with him by baptism into death." Rom. vi. 3, 4. For Paul says to the Colossians, "I now rejoice in my sufferings for you, and fill up that which is behind of the afflictions of Christ in my flesh, for his body's sake, which is the church." Col. i. 24. The true ministers of the gospel must, at times, be baptized into the states of the people, in order that they may minister to their wants; for the whole church is represented as one body and " whether one member suffer, all the members suffer with it; or one member be honoured, all the members rejoice with it. Now ye are the body of Christ," says the apostle, "and members in particular." 1 Cor. xii. 26. They who are willing thus to suffer and to labour in the cause of truth, offer up to God an acceptable sacrifice, whether it be in living to his glory, or in dying for his cause.

The prophecy of Isaiah (chap. liii.) which has been quoted, appears to have been understood in a figurative sense by the evangelist Matthew, and he has thrown much light upon the meaning of it. He says, "When the even was come, they brought unto him many that were possessed with devils; and he cast out the spirits with his word, and healed all that were sick: that it might be fulfilled which was spoken by Esaias the prophet, saying, Himself *took our infirmities*, and *bare our sicknesses*." Matthew viii. 16, 17.

Now let us inquire how he *took their infirmities*, and *bare their sicknesses*? Assuredly, not by becoming himself infirm and sick, nor by having his health imputed to them: but he "cast them out by his word," which was the "power of God and the wisdom of God." And in like manner the same Divine word, or power of God, still bears our iniquities; not by imputation, but by healing our spiritual diseases, and casting out every evil spirit from our minds, if we *have faith in him and obey his law.*

With these views, I can readily subscribe to all that is said of Christ in the New Testament; for it appears that not only his spotless life and powerful preaching, but still more the sublime example of his sufferings, were all calculated to operate upon the best feelings of mankind, and to bring them to the knowledge of God.

The doctrine that Jesus Christ suffered as a *substitute* for sinners, and paid the penalty of death that was denounced against Adam for transgression, is equally contrary to reason, and inconsistent with the scriptures. In the first place, it must be borne in mind, that the death which was denounced against Adam for transgression, was not the death of the natural body; or else it would have taken place agreeably to the prediction of the Most High,— "In *the day thou eatest thereof*, thou shalt surely die."

I have shown, in a former conversation, that this death did take place *at the time predicted*, and that it was a death in the soul; for, "to be *carnally minded is death.*" It was a being "dead in trespasses and sins,"—and it is evident that Jesus never did die this death, for he *never sinned*.

That he should suffer an outward death, in order to take away the effects of an inward one, is contrary both to reason and to scripture.*
"Shall I give my first born for my transgression?—the fruit of my body for the sin of my soul?" Micah vi. 7. Yet the authors of this doctrine would take the fruit of Adam's body, for the Messiah "was made of the seed of David [and consequently of Adam] according to the flesh," Rom. i. 3, and they would offer it up for the sin of Adam's soul! But let us suppose for a moment, that it was the death of the natural body that was denounced against Adam for transgression; did Christ's suffering in his

---

* This expression has been misunderstood. The author does not deny that spiritual blessings to mankind, have resulted from the obedience and sufferings of Christ, but he denies that Christ suffered as a *substitute* for sinners, or that his righteousness is *imputed* to sinners. "The righteousness of the righteous shall be upon him, and the wickedness of the wicked shall be upon him." Ezek. xviii. 20. "He that believeth is born of God, and he that is born of God is justified by Christ alone without *imputation*."—G. Fox: *Saul's Errand to Damascus*.

stead prevent him from dying? Certainly not: for "all the days that Adam lived were nine hundred and thirty years, and he died." And all his posterity continue to die, notwithstanding *the debt being paid* for us, according to this strange doctrine of man's invention.

James. I think that Jesus Christ is spoken of in the scriptures, as the "one mediator between God and man," and as "the mediator of the new covenant." What are we to understand by these expressions?

Father. This question may be answered in the language of George Fox, who says that "None know Him as a *mediator* and a lawgiver, nor an offering, nor his *blood* that cleanseth them, but as they know him working in them." Vol. 3, pp. 119, 120. As God is a spirit, and the soul of man is spiritual, it appears evident that the mediator (or medium of intercourse) between God and man must be spiritual.

The eternal word, or spirit of Christ revealed in the soul, is our advocate and our intercessor. For "the Spirit also helpeth our infirmities: for we know not what we should pray for as we ought, but the spirit itself *maketh intercession for us*, with groanings which cannot be uttered; and he that searcheth the hearts knoweth what is the mind of the spirit, because he *maketh intercession* for the saints according to the will of God." Rom. viii. 26, 27. "As the *word* manifested in the flesh, or become man, is the one mediator or restorer of union between God and man; so, to seeing eyes it must be evident, that nothing but this one mediatorial nature of Christ, *essentially brought to life in our souls*, can be our salvation through Christ Jesus. For *that* which *saved and exalted that humanity in which Christ* dwelt, *must* be the *salvation* of every human creature in the world." (See Law's Address to the Clergy, p. 51.) "It is the spirit, the body, the blood of Christ within us, that is our whole peace with God, our whole adoption, our whole redemption, our whole justification, our whole glorification; and this is the one thing said and meant by that new birth of which Christ saith, Except a man be born again from above he cannot enter into the kingdom of God. Now the true ground why all that is said of Christ in such a variety of expressions, hath only one meaning, and pointeth only to one and the same thing, is this : it is because the whole state and nature of fallen man wants only one thing, and that one thing is a real birth of the Divine nature, made living again in him as at the first: and then all is done that can be done, by all the mysteries of the birth and whole process of Christ for our salvation."

"All the law, the prophets, and the gospel are fulfilled, when there is in Christ a new creature, having life in and from him as really as the branch hath its life in and from the vine." (*Ibid.* p. 47.)

This union of the soul with God, by obedience to the manifestations of his spirit within us, is the whole sum and substance of the Christian religion. It was this which the blessed Messiah came to preach and exemplify; for the new covenant of which he was the minister, is not like the old law written upon tables of stone, but it is a spiritual law "placed in the mind and written in the heart;" therefore he said when he began to preach, "The spirit of the Lord is upon me, because he hath anointed me to preach the gospel to the poor; he hath sent me to heal the broken-hearted, to preach deliverance to the captives, and recovering of sight to the blind, to set at liberty them that are bruised, to preach the acceptable year of the Lord."— Luke iv. 18.

How plain and practical was his preaching! "The kingdom of God," said he, "cometh not with observation, for behold it is within you." "Except a man be born again, he cannot see the kingdom of God." The kingdom which he preached is a spiritual kingdom; it is the dominion of God established in the soul, bringing forth "righteousness, peace, and joy in the Holy Spirit." This practical and experimental part of religion is the only one in which the pious and faithful in all ages have agreed;—it is the only part that is essential to salvation; and the best evidence we can give of its possession is, by showing forth the fruits of righteousness in our life and conversation; for the tree will be known by its fruit.

CONVERSATION VI.

BAPTISM AND THE LORD'S SUPPER.

James. Since our last conversation, I have been reflecting on the subjects of baptism and the Lord's supper, which appear to have been ceremonies practised in the primitive Christian church, and are said to have been commanded by Christ himself. If they have such high authority for their observance, I do not see how any of the professed followers of Christ in the present day can disregard them.

Father. I am willing to state my views upon these subjects, and give the grounds on which my own convictions are founded; but I have seen so little good resulting from religious controversy, that I always abstain from it when possible. During the progress of an argument on any religious subject, the minds of both parties are generally too much excited to be open to conviction. Changes of sentiment on these subjects, are generally the result of deliberation, and communion with the witness of truth in our own consciences; and it often happens that the conclusions formed in this manner, although accompanied with sufficient weight of evidence for the satisfaction of our own minds, cannot be stated to others in such a manner as to satisfy them, until they shall have passed through the same stages of experience.

John. I think I can appreciate the soundness of this sentiment, for I know, by experience, that some religious truths which now appear very clear to my understanding, were at a former period the subject of much doubt; although I endeavoured to become acquainted with the strongest arguments that had been advanced for them, and felt a sincere desire to weigh them impartially. The subject of baptism is one on which my mind is not satisfied; and being desirous of conforming to all the commands of our Saviour, I have long been anxious for further light upon it.

Father. I have no doubt the Divine Master is now subjecting thee to the purifying process of his own baptism; and if thou art able to drink of the cup that he drank of, and to be baptized *with his baptism,* there will be no need of resorting to the outward and elementary type of that cleansing operation which his spirit performs within us.

James. I believe it is now agreed by most of those who administer water-baptism, that it makes no change in the heart, but is an outward and visible sign of an inward and invisible grace. They think it was commanded by Christ, and intended as a badge of our profession, and a seal of the covenant, as circumcision was given to the Israelites.

Father. I think if this were the case, we should find it mentioned in some of the writings of the New Testament; but it is not spoken of as the seal of the new covenant, nor can it be considered as the badge of Christian profession, because it leaves no impression to distinguish those who have received it from the rest of the world. The only seal of the new covenant is "the Holy Spirit, whereby *ye are sealed* unto the day of redemption:" (Eph. iv. 30) and the only badge of discipleship mentioned by the Divine Master, consists of the fruits which are produced by the influence of this spirit. "By this shall all men know that ye are my disciples, if ye have love one to another;" — and "Ye shall know them by their fruits."

John. The command of Christ to his disciples, "Go teach all nations, baptizing them in the name of the Father, and of the Son, and of the Holy Ghost," is considered by most persons as still obligatory upon the church.

Father. But in this text, *water*-baptism is not mentioned; and it appears that the writers of the New Testament speak of the baptism of John and that of Christ, as distinct from each other. John said to the Jews, "I indeed baptize you with water unto repentance, but he that cometh after me is mightier than I, whose shoes I am not worthy to bear, he shall baptize you with the *Holy Ghost and with fire;* whose fan is in his hand, and he will thoroughly purge his floor and gather his wheat into the garner, but he will burn up the chaff with unquenchable fire." Matt. iii. 11, 12. It is also said that when Paul came to Ephesus he found certain disciples, of whom he inquired, "Have ye received the Holy Ghost since ye believed? And they said unto him, We have not so much as heard whether there be any Holy Ghost. And he said unto them, Unto what then are ye baptized? And they said, Unto John's baptism.

Then said Paul, John baptized with the baptism of repentance, saying unto the people, That they should believe on him which should come after him, that is, on Christ Jesus. When they heard this, they were baptized in the name of the Lord Jesus. And when Paul had laid his hands upon them, the Holy Ghost came on them; and they spake with tongues, and prophesied. And all the men were about twelve." Acts xix. 2–7.

James. It seems to me that none can baptize with the Holy Ghost but Christ himself: and in the text just quoted, it appears that these new converts had been baptized with John's baptism unto repentance, and Paul had them baptized again in the name of the Lord Jesus; and after that he laid his hands on them, and they received the Holy Ghost. May we not conclude that Paul used water in this instance?

Father. I think not: for there were twelve of these disciples who were men; and Paul says in another place, that Christ had sent him not to baptize but to preach the gospel; and he thanked God that he had baptized none of them but Crispus and Gaius, and the household of Stephanus. 1 Cor. i. 14, 16. Although it may be said in one sense, that none can baptize with the spirit but Christ himself, the same may be said of preaching the gospel; which no man can do without Divine assistance. When the gospel is preached "in the demonstration of the spirit and of power," it has a baptizing influence; that is to say, it brings the hearers who are willing to receive it, under the influence of Divine love, and they become "baptized by one spirit into one body," and "are all made to drink into one spirit." 1 Cor. xii. 13. The apostles were not prepared for this spiritual baptism, until they had waited at Jerusalem, and were endued with power from on high, by the descending upon them of the Holy Ghost. And notwithstanding the miracles have ceased, which accompanied that baptism at the dawn of the gospel day,— yet the reality of it is as truly experienced *now*, by those who come under the influence of the spirit of Christ. Although Paul was not sent forth to baptize with water, there is no doubt his commission was as extensive as that of the other disciples; for he was clothed with Divine love, and was made instrumental in bringing others under its baptizing influence. This still continues to be the case with true gospel ministry, in proportion as the instrument is endowed with the ability which God giveth; for such ministry has always had a baptizing power.

John. But although water is not mentioned in these texts, there is another place where it is mentioned by Jesus himself. He said to Nicodemus, "Except a man be born of water and of the spirit, he cannot enter into the kingdom of God." John iii. 5.

Father. It must be observed, that on this occasion he had not been speaking of baptism, but of the *new birth;* and he goes on to say, "That which is born of the flesh is flesh, and that which is born of the Spirit is spirit." As the expression cannot be taken literally, it must be understood figuratively; that is, water being a purifying element, was coupled with the Spirit to describe its effects, in the same manner that fire was mentioned in conjunction with the Holy Spirit, by John the Baptist, when he said of Christ, "He shall baptize you with the Holy Ghost and with fire." Therefore the water here intended which can give a new birth, must be the water of the river of life, which whosoever drinketh shall never thirst.

James. But water-baptism was frequently, if not always, administered by the disciples, both before and after the crucifixion of Christ: and we know that Jesus himself submitted to the baptism of John.

Father. This argument, if valid in favour of water-baptism, is equally so with regard to circumcision, and other rituals of the Jewish law; to all of which the Messiah submitted.

We find that when Paul went up to Jerusalem, about twenty-seven years after the ascension of Christ, the disciples said to him, "Thou seest, brother, how many thousands of Jews there are which believe, and they are all *zealous of the law.*" And Paul condescended to their prejudices so far as to purify himself, and to enter with four others into the temple, " until an offering should be offered for every one of them." It appears further, that Peter was so filled with Jewish prejudices, eight years after the ascension of Christ, that it required a remarkable vision to convince him that he ought to go unto the house of Cornelius to preach the gospel; and after he had done so, " they of the circumcision contended with him, saying, Thou wentest in unto men uncircumcised, and didst eat with them."

I mention these circumstances to show, that even the apostles, as well as the other Jewish converts to Christianity, did not at once come into the spirituality of the gospel dispensation, but retained for a considerable time a number of the Jewish rites and ceremonies; and no doubt they adhered with equal fondness to the water-baptism of John. It is said of Apollos, that being "fervent in the spirit, he taught diligently the things of the Lord, *knowing only the baptism of John.* And he began to speak boldly in the synagogue; whom when Aquila and Priscilla had heard, they took him unto them, and expounded unto him the word of God more perfectly." Acts xviii. 25, 26.

John. It is said in the scriptures, that the disciples administered water-baptism while the Master was with them; consequently we may suppose he did not disapprove of it.

Father. In this passage it is stated, "When therefore the Lord knew how the Pharisees had heard that Jesus made and baptized more disciples than John, (though Jesus himself baptized not, but his disciples,) he left Judea and departed again into Galilee." John iv. 1, etc. John was at that time baptizing in or near Ænon, *where there was much water;* and I have no doubt the disciples were influenced by his example, and by that activity in religious performances which new converts are apt to exhibit;

but it appears that Jesus himself did not engage in it, nor would it have been consistent with his mission to have taken up the baptism of John, which was only a type of his own spiritual baptism; therefore, when he knew the report which the Pharisees had heard, he removed into another place.

James. It is, however, asserted, that the practice of the Christian churches, from the time of the apostles down to the present day, has (with the single exception of the Society of Friends,) been all in favour of water-baptism, either by sprinkling or immersion.

Father. John the Baptist said of Christ, "He must increase, but I must decrease;" which no doubt alluded to the two dispensations which they administered: and accordingly it has always been found, that the more completely the mind is brought under the purifying and baptizing power of Christ, the less dependence is placed upon any outward rite or ceremony. Of this we have a remarkable example in the apostle Paul, who saw beyond the types and shadows of a former dispensation, and perceived that the spiritual kingdom of Christ contained the substance of them all.

The service under the Mosaic law, "stood

only in meats and drinks, and divers washings, and cardinal ordinances, imposed on them *until the time of reformation.*" Heb. ix. 10. Therefore, this experienced apostle says, "Let no man judge you in meat or in drink, or in respect of a holy day, or of the new moon, or of the sabbath days; which are a shadow of things to come; but the body is of Christ." Col. ii. 16, 17. "Wherefore, if ye be dead with Christ from the rudiments of the world, why, as though living in the world, are ye *subject to ordinances* (touch not, taste not, handle not, which all are to perish with the using) after the commandments and doctrines of men? Which things have indeed a show of wisdom in will-worship and humility, and neglecting of the body; not in any honour to the satisfying of the flesh." Ver. 20–23.

Paul expressed his thankfulness that he had used water-baptism but in a few instances, which he mentioned; because he was not sent forth to administer this ceremony, but to preach the gospel, and to bring men under the baptizing power of the Holy Spirit. He says, there is "*One* Lord, *one* faith, *one* baptism, one God and Father of all, who is above all, and through all, and in you all." Eph. iv. 5, 6. Now, if there be but *one baptism* that saves, can we be at any loss to know which it is?—whether the water-baptism of John, or the spiritual baptism of Christ?

In the infancy of the Christian church, the Jewish converts were nearly all "zealous of the law" of Moses; and we have reason to believe that it had long been the practice, under that law, for the converts from heathenism to wash their bodies in water, as a sign of purification; and this ceremony being further confirmed by the dispensation of John the Baptist, it was still retained in the infancy of the Christian church; although there is no doubt that others besides the apostle Paul, saw that it was not essential to the Christian dispensation.*

After the apostles and elders of the church were removed by death, those who succeeded them showed a great disposition to multiply rites and ceremonies; some of which (as historians inform us) were adopted from the Mosaic

---

* In the scriptures there is no instance mentioned of infants being subjected to water-baptism, nor indeed of adults born of Christian parents. It may be inferred from 1 Cor. vii. 14, that the children of believing parents were considered members of the church.

law, and some were copied from the heathen festivals, in order to ingratiate themselves and recommend their religion to the multitude.

During the earlier ages of the church, water-baptism was administered by immersion, and to adults only;—but in after-times, when the doctrine of original sin had been introduced by the vain speculations of philosophers, they began to baptize infants, in order to wash away the sin supposed to be inherited from Adam; and as these infants could not answer for themselves, godfathers and godmothers were introduced to answer for them, and to promise that they should renounce the devil and all his works. The sprinkling of infants and the promises of godfathers and godmothers, are now considered by the reflecting part of the community as mere lifeless ceremonies, having no warrant in the scriptures, nor in the practice of the primitive church.

It must be acknowledged, however, that the baptism of adults by immersion in water, was practised in the days of the apostles; but it was not administered nor commanded by Jesus Christ, neither is it a part of his spiritual dispensation; although, like circumcision and other Jewish ceremonies, it was permitted to continue for a season, and was known among the disciples by the name of "*John's baptism*," which was intended to decrease as that of Christ should increase.

The *baptism which saves*, is spoken of by the apostles as an inward, spiritual washing; "not the putting away of the filth of the flesh, but the answer of a good conscience towards God, by the resurrection of Jesus Christ." 1 Pet. iii. 21.—"Not by works of righteousness which we have done, but according to his mercy he *saved us, by the washing of regeneration*, and renewing of the Holy Ghost." Titus iii. 5. "Christ also loved the church, and gave himself for it, that he might sanctify and cleanse it with the washing of *water by the word*." Eph. v. 25, 26. "But ye are washed, but ye are sanctified, but ye are justified in the name of the Lord Jesus, and by the spirit of our God." 1 Cor vi. 11.

I believe there are few intelligent minds in the present age and in our country, who will contend that any change is produced in the soul by water-baptism, or that the favour of God can be secured by such a ceremony. How can we suppose that a just and merciful Creator would regard with more favour an infant whose parents have subjected it to this process, than one that had died without it? In either case, there can be no merit accruing to the infant; because it exercises no choice in the matter, and incurs no responsibility thereby. If, therefore, it makes no difference in the case of infants, dying without baptism, it can make none with those adults who believe that water-baptism was not commanded by Jesus Christ, nor intended to be perpetuated in his church. Such persons may safely say of water-baptism, as the apostle Paul said of circumcision, "In Christ Jesus neither circumcision availeth any thing, nor uncircumcision, but a new creature." And furthermore, if we see any of these persons who manifest by a life and conversation consistent with godliness, that they are servants of the Most High, and enjoy his favour; is not this an evidence that he looks only at the heart, and that outward ceremonies are of no avail in securing his approbation?

John. This reasoning will apply equally well to all outward ceremonies, and especially to that of the Lord's supper; yet there appears to be a command of our Saviour for the observance of this ceremony, where he says, "This do in remembrance of me."

Father It is true that he eat the *passover* with his disciples; but there is no evidence that he intended it to be perpetuated in the church; nor is there any reason to suppose that he instituted a new ceremony on that occasion. He sent two of his disciples, saying, "Go into the city to such a man and say unto him, I will keep the passover at thy house with my disciples." Now we know that the paschal lamb which was eaten on this occasion, was instituted to commemorate the salvation of the Israelites, when the first-born of the Egyptians were slain by the destroying angel.

This lamb was also a figure of the meek and spotless nature of "Christ our passover,"—"the Lamb of God that taketh away the sins of the world." As in the outward passover, the blood was sprinkled on the door-posts, and they eat standing, with their loins girded, as men prepared for a journey; and with the lamb they partook of unleavened bread: so with the antitype, the spiritual body and blood of Christ, which is *the life and power that dwelt in him*, it is only those who partake of it that are saved by it; and we must receive it as those who are prepared for a journey to the promised land, and with "the unleavened bread of sincerity and truth." 1 Cor. v. 8.

Previous to this memorable occasion, the Divine Master had instructed his disciples in the nature of that spiritual food which nourishes the soul unto everlasting life, saying, "I am the living bread which came down from heaven." "He that eateth my flesh and drinketh my blood, dwelleth in me, and I in him." John vi. 51, 56. This language offended many who understood it literally,—but to his disciples he explained it by saying, "The flesh profiteth nothing, it is the *spirit that quickeneth:* the words that I speak unto you, they are spirit, and they are life."

James. But may we not suppose that he intended the bread and wine which were used at the last supper, to be perpetuated in the church as symbols or figures of his flesh and blood? for they are not only mentioned by the evangelists, but by the apostle Paul, who says, "I have received of the Lord that which also I delivered unto you, That the Lord Jesus, the same night in which he was betrayed, took bread: and when he had given thanks, he brake it, and said, Take, eat; this is my body, which is broken for you: this do in remembrance of me. After the same manner also he took the cup, when he had supped, saying, This cup is the new testament in my blood; this do ye as oft as ye drink it, in remembrance of me: for as often as ye eat this bread and drink this cup, ye do show forth the Lord's death till he come." 1 Corinth. xi. 23–26.

Father. All the ceremonies of the Mosaic law were observed by Jesus Christ; for that law was not abrogated till after his crucifixion. The passover was one of these ceremonies, and had a more immediate reference to himself than any of the others. It is not surprising then that he should, while celebrating this feast, endeavour to turn the attention of his followers to the spiritual meaning of it, by speaking of that bread which comes down from heaven and nourishes the soul; and of that wine which he would drink new with them in his Father's kingdom. He told them, as oft as they eat and drank, to do it in remembrance of him, and thereby they would show forth his death *till he came.* But did he not come to them again to rule and to reign in them, when, after waiting at Jerusalem, they were all baptized with the Holy Spirit? This was the fulfilment of his promise: " I will not leave you comfortless,—I will come to you," and "Lo! I am with you alway, even unto the end of the world." This was to them the second appearance of Christ. And to every regenerated soul he still appears in spirit, and is that substance and life which fulfils all the shadows and ceremonies of the law, and sets free from them.

Moses, when he gave forth the outward law, was exceedingly particular as to the time and manner in which every ceremony should be performed. He also left written directions respecting it, and instituted an order of priests and Levites to perform the service of the altar, and to explain the law to the people.

But when Jesus Christ came to introduce the new covenant dispensation, he prescribed no outward ceremonies, nor did he institute any order of priests. Let us read his admirable sermon on the mount, which is the clearest exposition we have of his doctrines, and we shall there find nothing that would lead us to place reliance upon rites or ceremonies of any kind. Nothing short of purity of heart and uprightness of conduct, can render us acceptable with God. When he was about to leave his disciples, he told them "to wait at Jerusalem until they should be endued with power from on high." "For John truly baptized with water, but ye shall be baptized with the Holy Ghost not many days hence." Acts i. 5. "I have many things to say unto you, but ye cannot bear them now. Howbeit, when he, the Spirit of Truth, is come, he will guide you into all truth." John xvi. 12, 13.

I therefore conclude, that as Jesus Christ "blotted out the hand-writing of ordinances that was against us, which was contrary to us, and took it out of the way, nailing it to his cross," Col. ii. 14,— he did not intend to introduce in its stead another ceremonial religion; but to lead his followers to the spiritual reality of communion with God. "We are of the circision," said the apostle Paul, "who worship God in the spirit, and have no confidence in the flesh."

James. It appears from the history of the church, that the supper was celebrated by the primitive Christians, and the sacrament is still in use among almost every portion of the Christian Church.

Father. It is true that we have accounts of the supper being eaten by the primitive Christians; but the ceremony now observed of eating a wafer and drinking of wine, is not a supper either as to time or form.

Mosheim informs us, that "both the Asiatic churches and those of Rome fasted during the great week, (so that was called in which Christ died,) and afterwards celebrated, *like the Jews, a sacred feast;* at which they distributed a *paschal lamb,* in memory of the holy supper." The eastern and western churches differed about the time and manner of observing this ceremony; and it occasioned many bitter disputes, and much bloodshed, after the church became corrupted. If the supper which Christ partook of with his disciples, and which was imitated by the primitive churches, was intended to be observed by succeeding generations, who has a right to alter its form, or to omit some of its most interesting features, or to substitute in its place another ceremony? Yet it has been altered, or entirely changed, by all the reformed churches, with the exception of the Menonists, and United Brethren.

When Jesus had celebrated the passover with his disciples, "he took a towel and poured water into a basin, and began to wash his disciples' feet, and to wipe them with the towel wherewith he was girded. Peter saith unto him, Thou shalt never wash my feet; Jesus answered him, If I wash thee not, thou hast no part with me. Simon Peter saith unto him, Lord, not my feet only, but also my hands and my head. Jesus saith unto him, He that is washed needeth not, save to wash his feet, but is clean every whit; and ye are clean but not all. For he knew who would betray him; therefore said he, Ye are not all clean. So after he had washed their feet, and had taken his garments and was set down again, he said unto them, Know ye what I have done to you? Ye call me Master and Lord, and ye say well, for so I am. If I then, your Lord and Master, have washed your feet, ye also ought to wash one another's feet; for I have given you an example, that ye should do as I have done to you." John xiii. 4–15.

Now, this part of the ceremony is fully as instructive as the rest, and was even more explicitly enjoined upon the disciples; yet it is entirely omitted by nearly the whole of professing Christendom. Instead of washing one another's feet, they sprinkle a little water in the face, and call it baptism; and instead of eating the paschal lamb in the evening, they partake of a wafer in the middle of the day.

James. It appears to me, that if these ceremonies are to be observed at all, they ought to be performed precisely as described in the scriptures; and not only these, but the anointing of the sick, and every other ceremony observed by the primitive Christians. We shall be much more excusable for considering them all as types, which were permitted for a season, but intended to be laid aside in the further progress of the church, than to select those which are most agreeable to ourselves, and to neglect or modify the others.

Father. There is much allowance to be made for the early Christians, in their fondness for ceremonial worship. The first converts were chiefly Jews, who had been accustomed from their infancy to the imposing rites of the old law, which had been enjoined upon them by the Most High through his servant Moses. Although the Messiah came to fulfil and to abrogate that law, we do not find any account in the scriptures, that he prohibited the observance of it. But by instructing them in the spiritual nature of this kingdom, and directing their attention to the teachings of the Spirit of Truth, which would lead them into all truth, he prepared the way for them to come out from their "bondage under the elements of the world," "that they might receive the adoption of sons." Gal. iv. 3, 5.

In the spiritual appearance of Christ, which is the establishment of Divine power in the hearts of his people, all the types and shadows of the old law and of John's dispensation, are fulfilled. By this means the soul becomes purified and " washed in the laver of regeneration," "in the name of the Lord Jesus, and by the spirit of our God." It also feeds upon the hidden manna, the body and blood of Christ, which are the substance and the life that come down from heaven, and give life to the soul. These can say with the apostle, "The cup of blessing which we bless, is it not the communion of the blood of Christ? the bread which we break, is it not the communion of the body of Christ? for we, *being many, are one bread and one body*, for we are all partakers of that one bread." 1 Cor. x. 16, 17. This can only be true of those who become members of that spiritual body of which Christ is the head. For, as in the animal body, every member is animated with the same life, and the same blood circulates through every part, and supplies nourishment to all; so in the spiritual relation, — the members, though many, are all partakers of *one bread* and form but *one body.* "Behold, I stand at the door and knock," says Christ: "if any man hear my voice, and open the door, I will come in to him, and will sup with him, and he with me." Rev. iii, 20. This is indeed the banquet of the soul, in which the new wine of the kingdom and the bread of life, are distributed to nourish the soul unto everlasting life.

I believe there are those among every sect and denomination, who come to partake of this spiritual food; but many of these are so far influenced by education and tradition, as to believe it necessary for them to observe the typical ceremonies, which were instituted in a darker age, and given to a superficial people. May we not say to these sincere professors, as Paul said to the Galatians, "Received ye the spirit by the works of the law, or by the hearing of faith? Are ye so foolish? having begun in the Spirit, are ye now made perfect by the flesh?" Gal. iii. 2, 3. "Let no man, therefore, judge you in meat, or in drink, or in respect of a holy day, or of the new moon, or of the Sabbath days,—which are a shadow of things to come, but the body is of Christ." Col. ii. 16.

Let us consider whether we have not a testimony to bear against many of those outward rites and ceremonies, which may have been instituted as signs of a gospel day to come:—but if that day has come, or if the "night is far spent, and the day is at hand," let us prepare ourselves to turn away from the shadows, and walk in the light, that we may be "children of the light and of the day" of pure posgel substance.

www.ingramcontent.com/pod-product-compliance
Lightning Source LLC
Chambersburg PA
CBHW020823230426

43666CB00007B/1078